## UNREAL AUTOS
INCREDIBLE CARS, STERLING REPARTEE

UNREAL AUTOS
PRESENTS

THE BEST CAR BOOK
IN THE WORLD

200 pages of unbelievable cars

Unreal Autos, United Kingdom
www.unrealautos.com

Author's & Typographical copyright © 2014 Unreal Autos

Unreal Autos asserts copyright over this work worldwide including the UK, US and EU.

All rights reserved. No part of this publication may be reproduced, stored in a retrieval system, or transmitted, in any form or by any means, without the prior permission in writing of Unreal Autos, or as expressly permitted by law, or under terms agreed with the appropriate reprographics rights organization.

First Unreal Autos edition published 2014

Printed in the United States of America and the United Kingdom 10 9 8 7 6 5 4 3 2 1

A catalogue record for this book is available from the British Library

ISBN XXX-X-XXX-XXXXX-X (Hardback)
ISBN 978-1-494-95769-8 (Paperback)
ISBN XXX-X-XXX-XXXXX-X (PDF)
ISBN XXX-X-XXX-XXXXX-X (EPUB) ISBN XXX-X-XXX-XXXXX-X (Kindle)

Unreal Autos and the Unreal Autos logos are trademarks owned by Peter Hedditch.

# CONTENTS

1. Top 10 World's Most Outrageous Supercar Designs — 12
2. Top 10 Most Expensive Cars of 2013 — 39
3. Top 5 Most Valuable Cars in the World — 65
4. 10 Important Milestones in Automotive History — 78
5. The World's Coolest Concept Cars — 86
6. Top 5 Futuristic Cars from Sci-fi Films — 112
7. When Will We Have a Flying Car? — 129
8. Top 10 Tips from Professional Racers — 144
9. Top 5 In-car Gadgets — 169
10. Top 10 Most Beautiful Cars Ever Made — 182

www.unrealautos.com

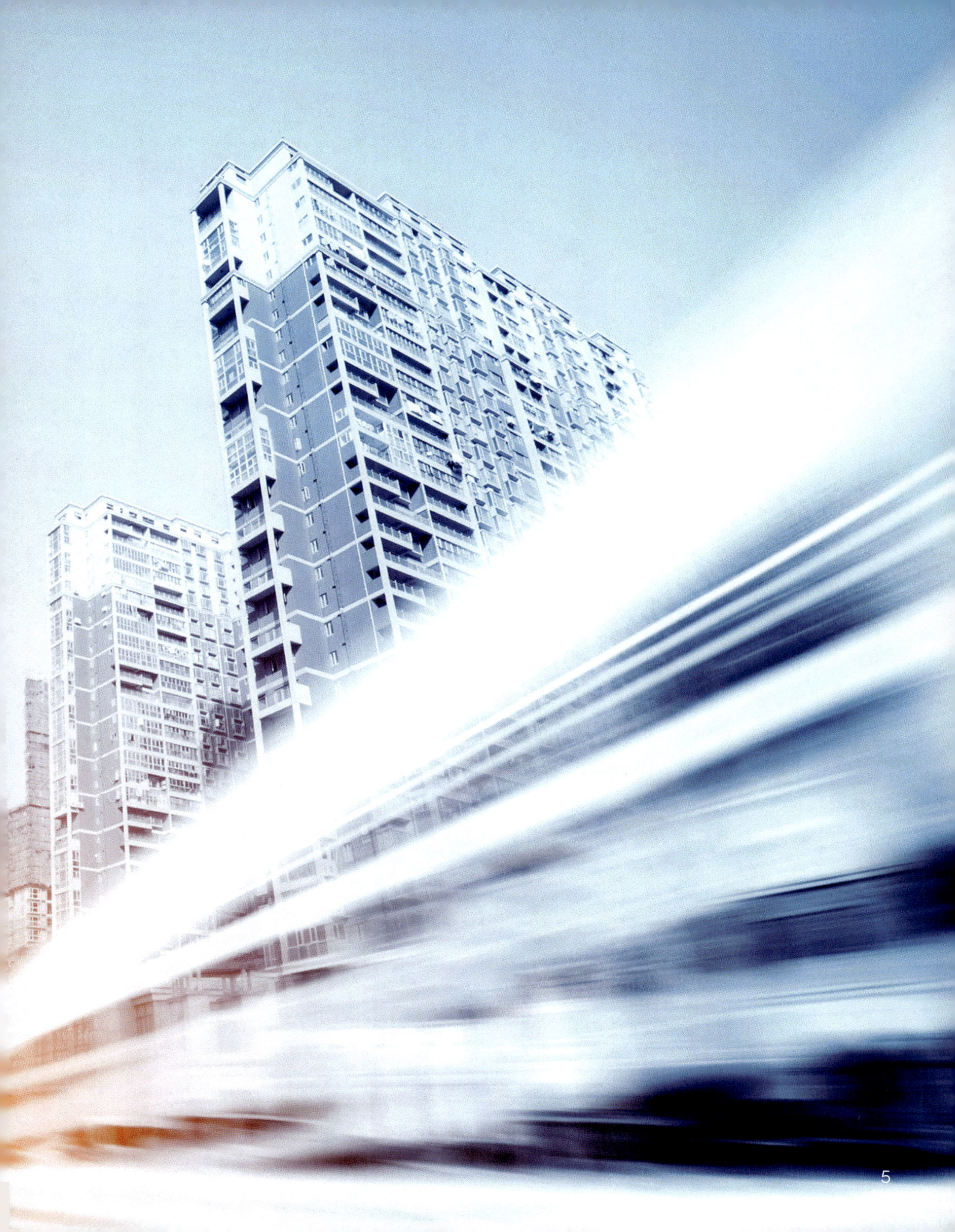

# PREPARE YOURSELF
## FOR THE JOURNEY OF A LIFETIME...

www.unrealautos.com

7

www.unrealautos.com

# THROUGH THE WORLD'S MOST STUNNINGLY BEAUTIFUL PLACES

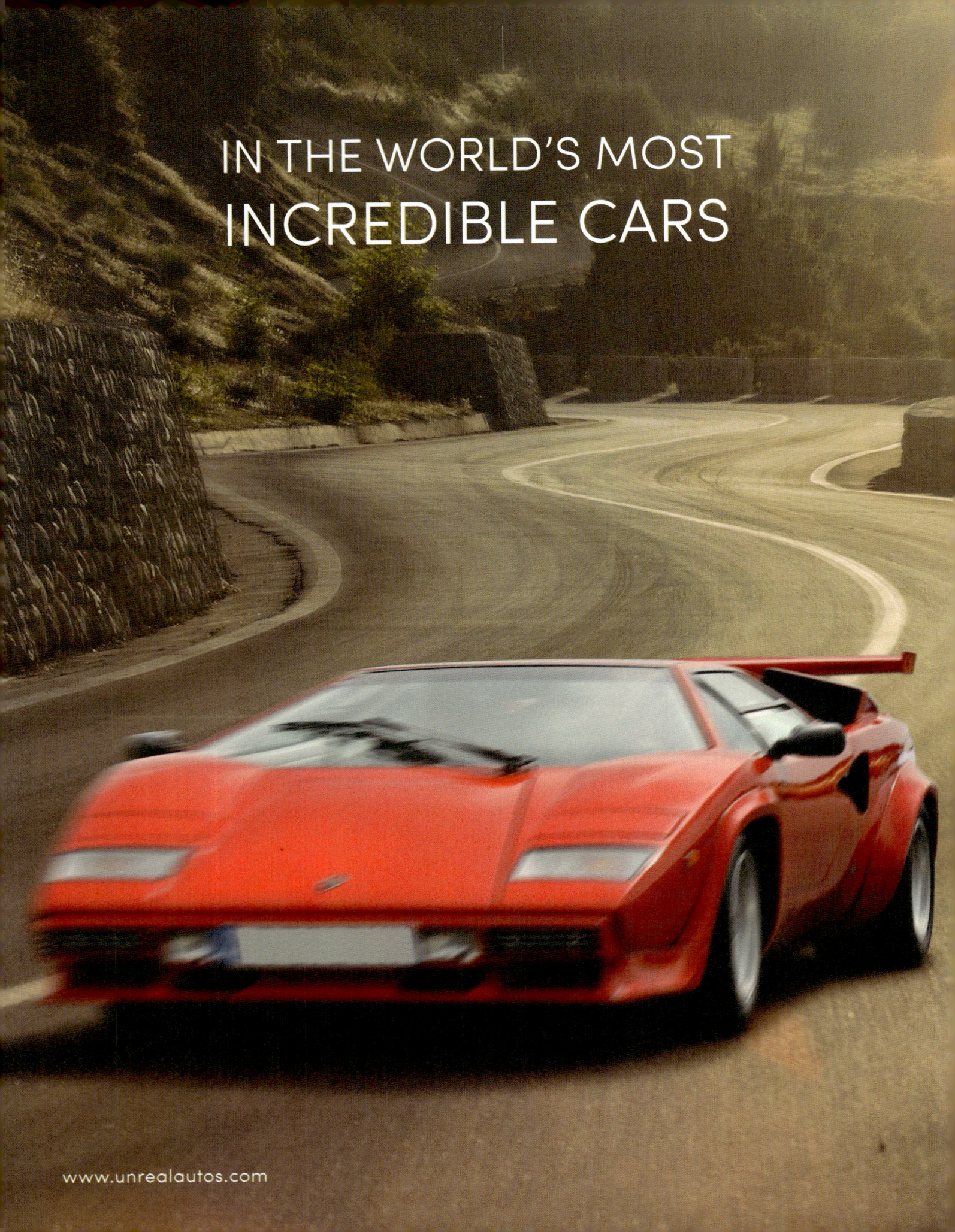

# IN THE WORLD'S MOST
# INCREDIBLE CARS

www.unrealautos.com

Unreal Autos opens a door into the world of the rich, the glamorous, the sublime and the ridiculous, and takes you on a rubber-burning journey through the milestones of automotive greatness.

Prepare to be amazed as you get close up with the supercar, the pioneer, the concept car and the ultra-expensive.

Driving is changing, technology is striding forward, and challenges lie on the horizon, but we haven't lost our love for the motorcar, or for the sheer thrill and adventure of the experience.

So fasten your seatbelts and feast your eyes on this full-colour guide to the world's top motors, past, present and future – and don't forget to check your wing mirrors. It's time for some very beautiful and very unreal autos.

CHAPTER 1
# TOP 10 MOST OUTRAGEOUS SUPERCAR DESIGNS

Supercars might be outrageous because of their shape, materials, power, or all of the above. One manufacturer seems to be making a habit of churning out artistic shock statements – but we'll let you work that out for yourself!

Anyone can draw something outrageous but it's another thing to make it a reality. So to make it onto our Top 10 all-time outrageous supercar designs, there has to have been at least one complete prototype actually built.

THE 2013 PEUGEOT ONYX

# 10.

## SSC TUATARA
### (2011 PROTOTYPE)

Shelby Super Cars (SSC) have come up with some record-breaking motors, and are flying the flag for the American supercar industry. It's not often we show you a car's back-end but in this case we make an exception. Serious tail features!

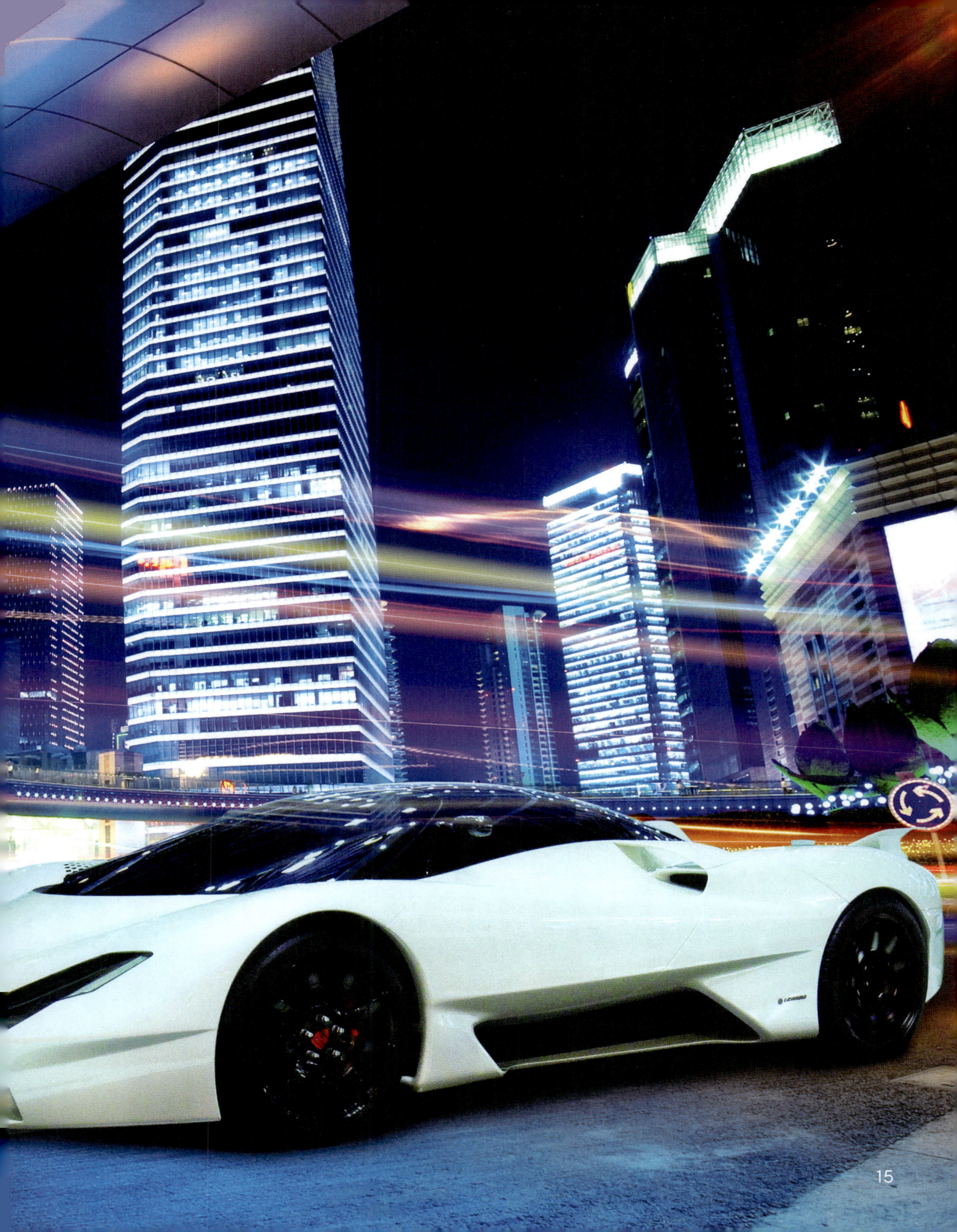

# 9.
## LAMBORGHINI SESTO ELEMENTO

The sixth element in the periodic table is carbon and the obsessive extent to which Lambo have used the grey stuff in this car earns it a place in our Top 10. Then, of course, there are those eyebrow-raising red bonnet triangles.

www.unrealautos.com

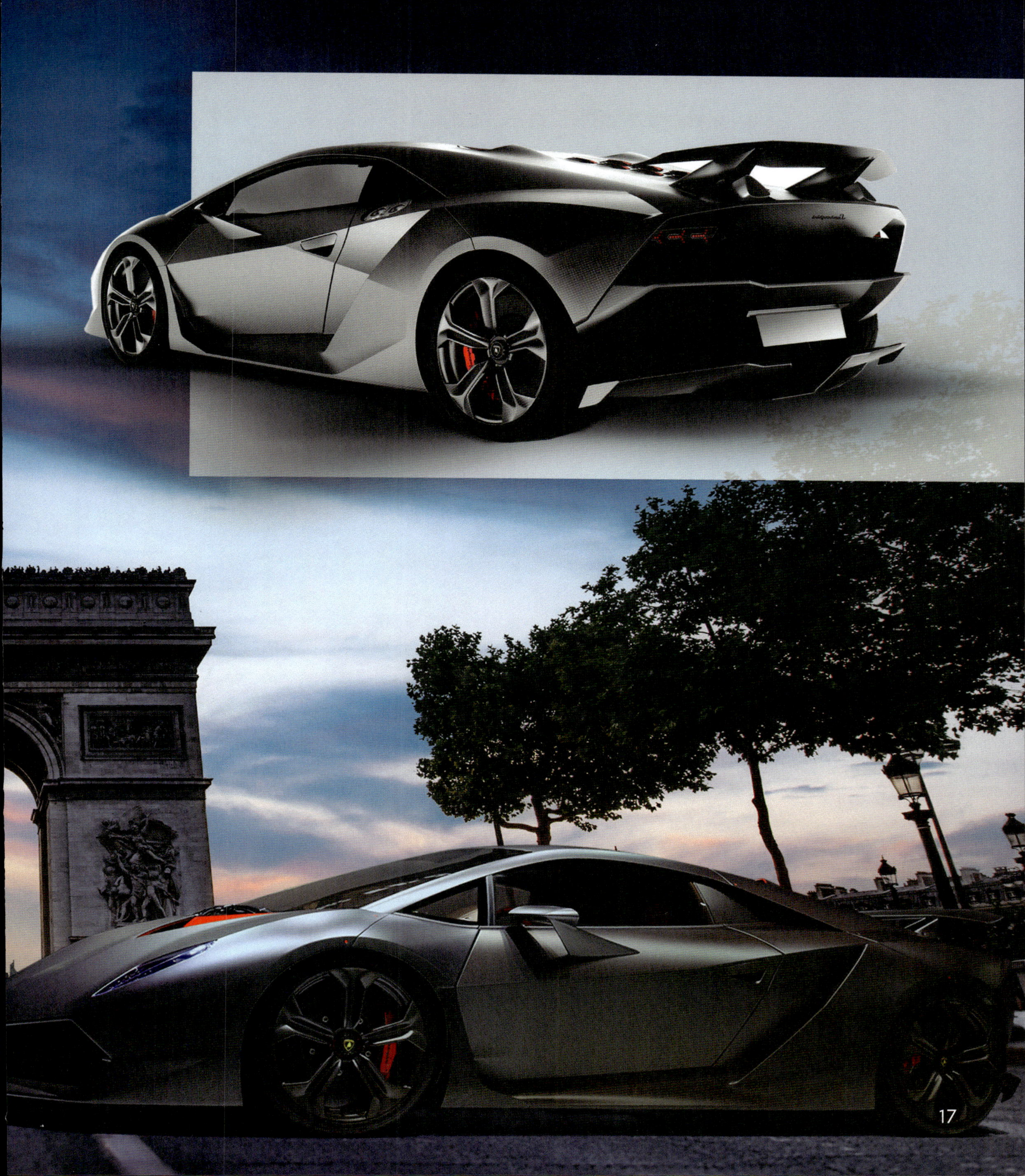

# 8.

## MERCEDES-BENZ SLR MCLAREN STIRLING MOSS

While the SLR McLaren was really just a grand tourer, the Stirling Moss edition is a supercar racing variant with no roof or windscreen – which is fairly outrageous. It also boasted a higher top speed at 220mph.

www.unrealautos.com

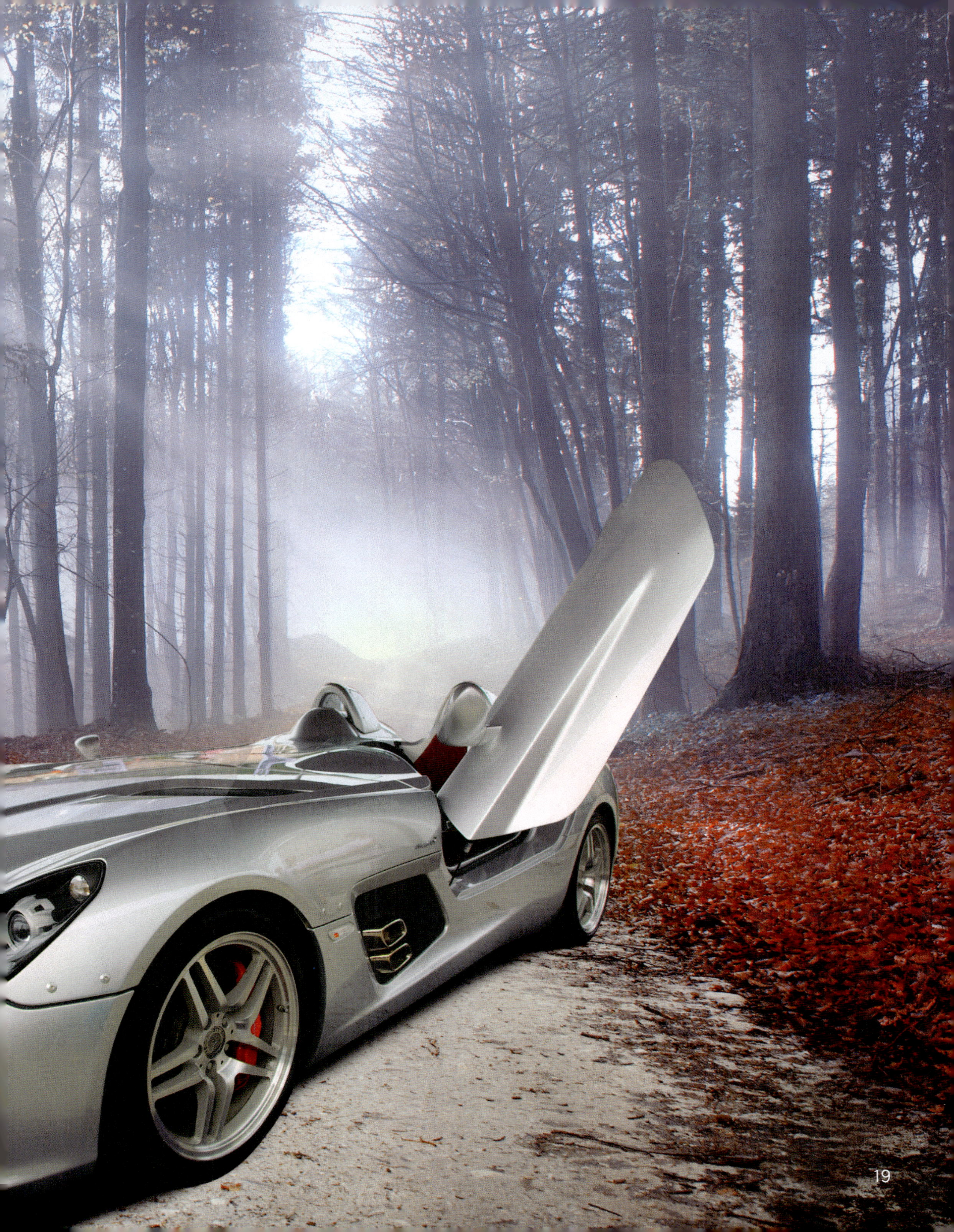

# 7.
## PEUGEOT ONYX (2013)

What is more shocking? A car with copper plating designed to turn green over time, a recycled newspaper dashboard, or the fact that both of these are found in a Peugeot of all things? Oh, and the tail lights up blue when you close the doors.

www.unrealautos.com

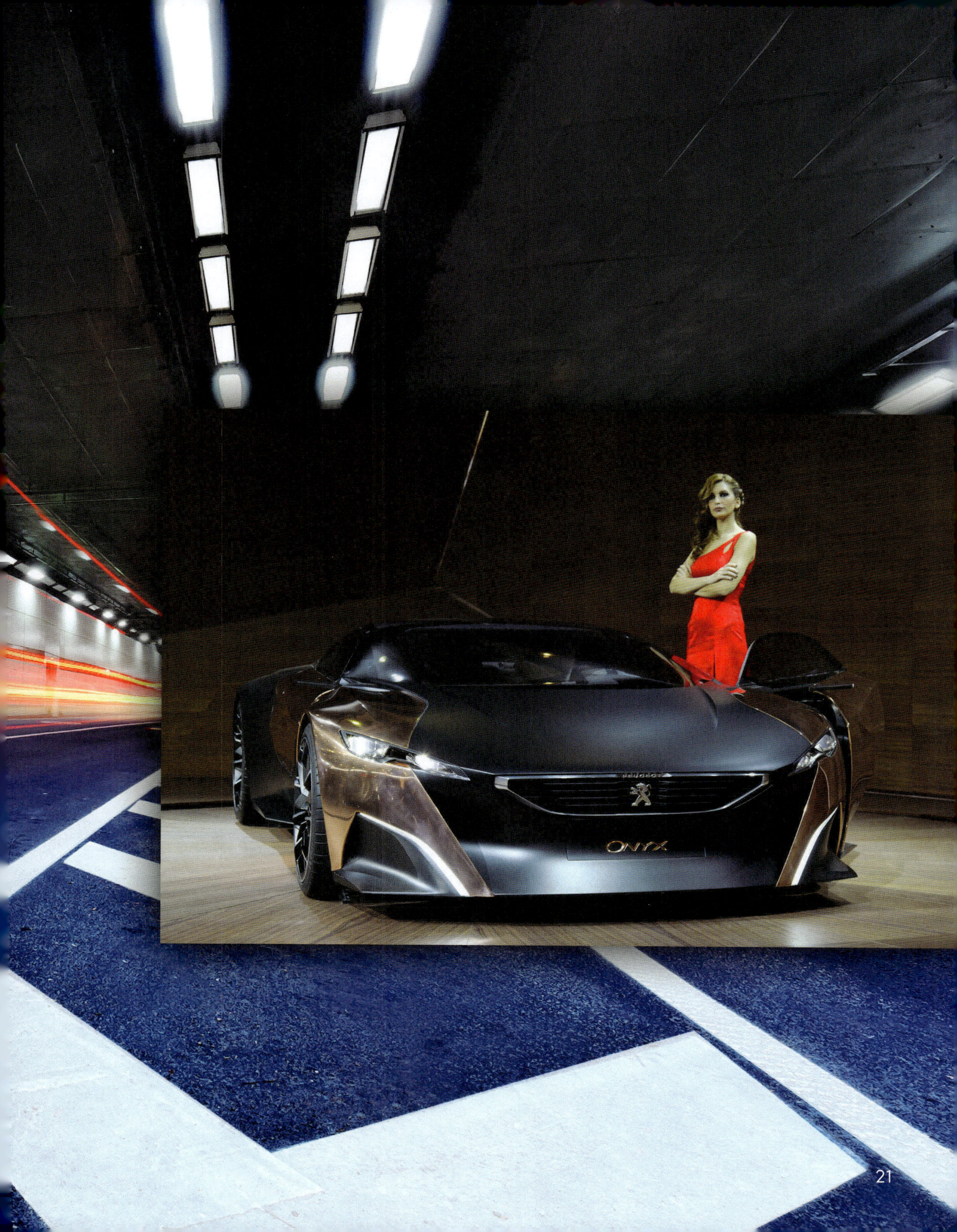
ONYX

## 6. BUGATTI VEYRON EB 16.4 SUPER SPORTS (2010)

Outrageously powerful, the clue is in the name, 16.4 meaning 16 cylinders and quad-turbocharged. When the original 8-litre Veyron lost its speed crown to the SSC Ultimate Aero, Bugatti came up with a new 1,184bhp version to take it back.

www.unrealautos.com

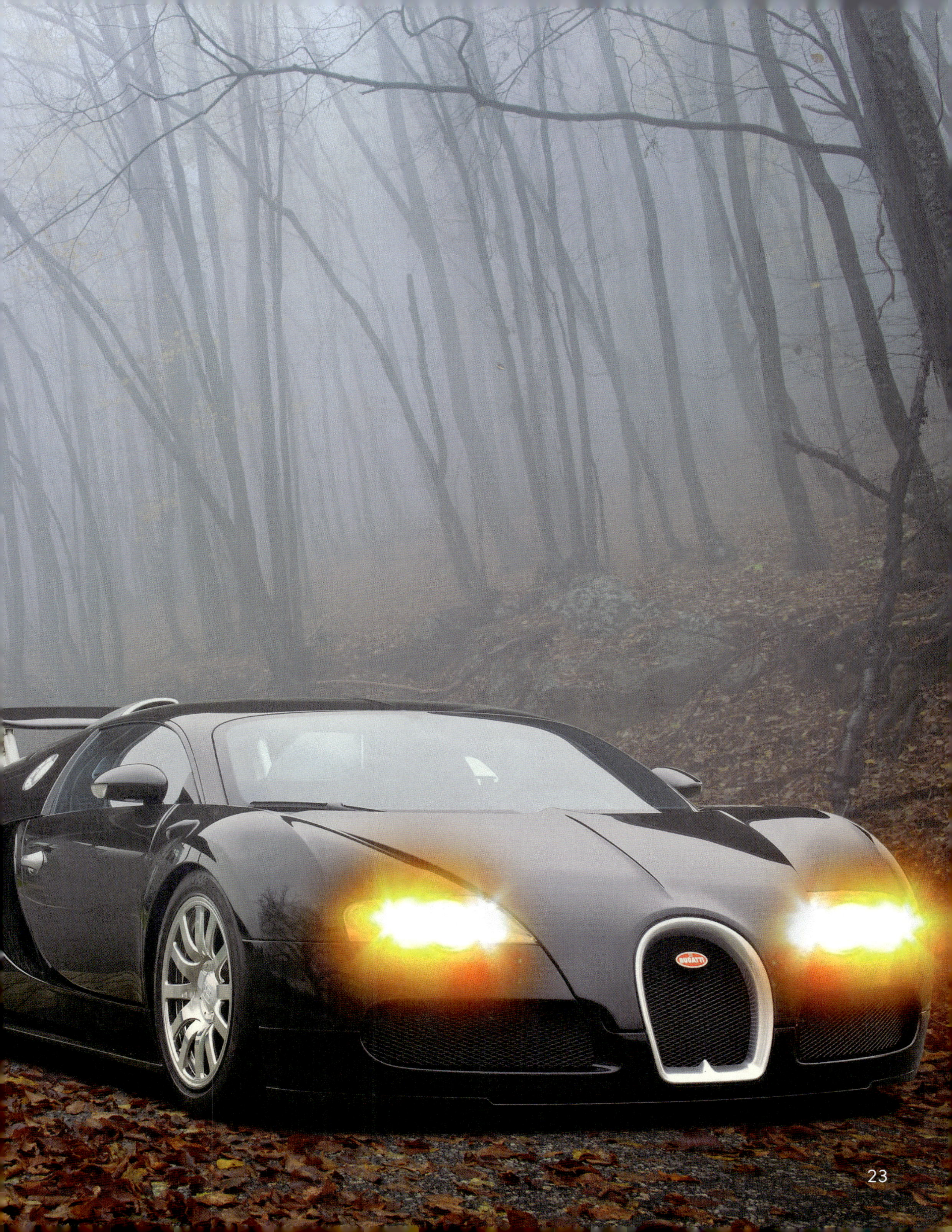

www.unrealautos.com

# 5.
## DEVEL SIXTEEN
## (2013)

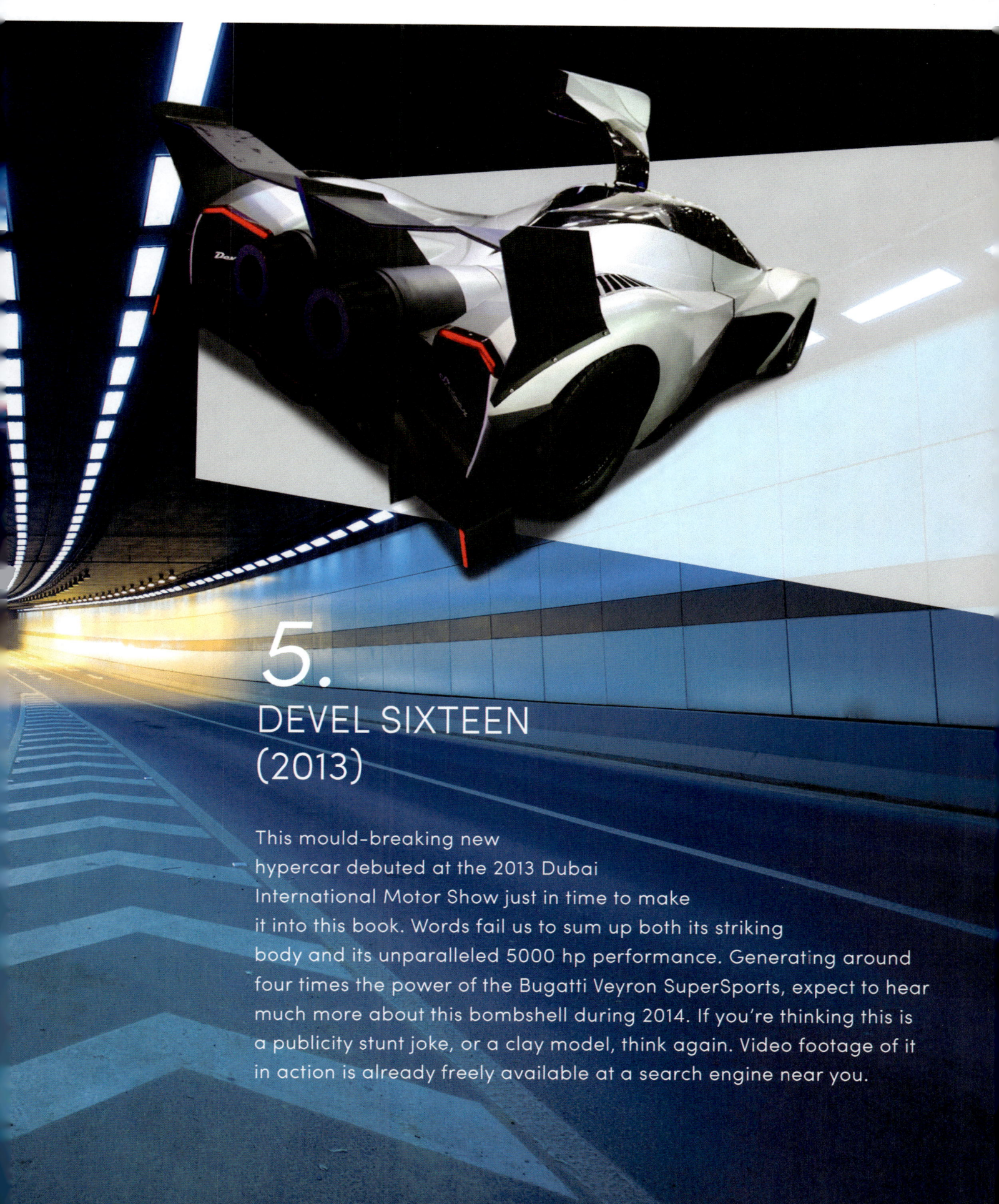

This mould-breaking new hypercar debuted at the 2013 Dubai International Motor Show just in time to make it into this book. Words fail us to sum up both its striking body and its unparalleled 5000 hp performance. Generating around four times the power of the Bugatti Veyron SuperSports, expect to hear much more about this bombshell during 2014. If you're thinking this is a publicity stunt joke, or a clay model, think again. Video footage of it in action is already freely available at a search engine near you.

www.unrealautos.com

## 4. LAMBORGHINI COUNTACH (1974)

So low you have to be a limbo dancer to get in; so restrictive on the window movement, you can't get a half-pound burger through the gap at a drive-in, the Countach is the stuff of design legend.

DOWNLOAD THESE PHOTOS AS DESKTOP WALLPAPERS OR POSTERS
Go to www.unrealautos.com/wallpapers

# 3.
## LANCIA STRATOS ZERO (1970)

Uncompromising wedge-shaped looks mean that the Zero actually had very little in common with the rallying Stratos HF. Just look at that thin line of lights in the front bumper. It's like a razor's edge!

www.unrealautos.com

29

www.unrealautos.com

## 2. LAMBORGHINI PREGUNTA (1998)

Only one V12 roadster was built and any car that requires you to stop and think which end is the front must be fairly outrageous. By the way, Pregunta is Spanish for question.

www.unrealautos.com

# 1. LAMBORGHINI EGOISTA (2013)

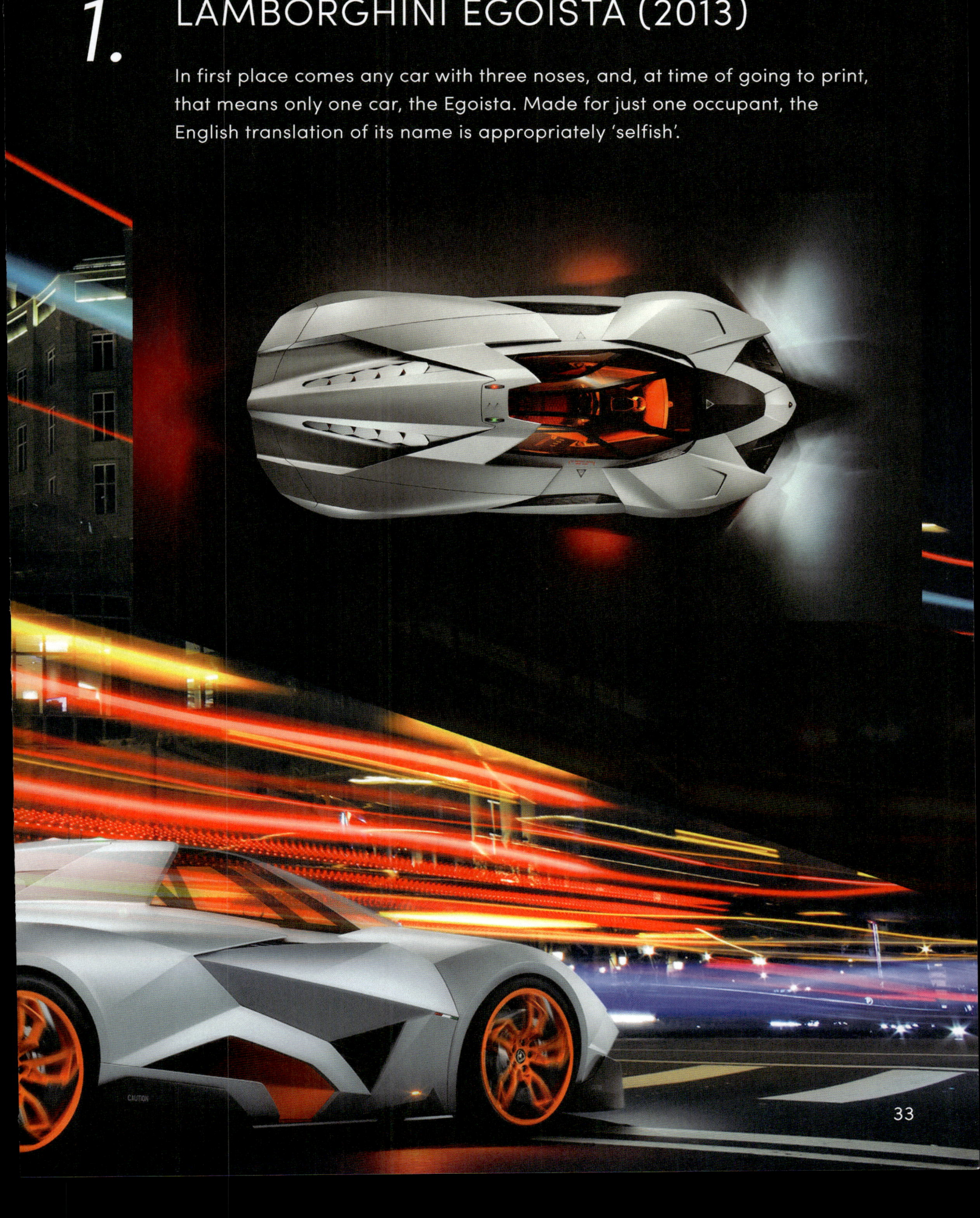

In first place comes any car with three noses, and, at time of going to print, that means only one car, the Egoista. Made for just one occupant, the English translation of its name is appropriately 'selfish'.

# Did you know?

Car manufacturer Henry Ford only offered his customers cars in one colour, black, because it was the cheapest to use, quickest to dry, and the most durable. Also, by only offering one colour, the production line was uniform and the vehicle price kept as low as possible.

Some say, Kevin Costner is the reincarnation of Henry Ford -- movie coming soon?

Ford have come a long way since the Model T philosophy

www.unrealautos.com

There's nothing so unforgiving
As the crannies of a car
For losing some keys
Or a chocolate bar

Over hill and down dale
Over seat and down foot-well
Your efforts will fail
And the car remains keeper

Why did I have to put it in my trouser pocket?
Is something burning in the lighter socket?

www.unrealautos.com

## CHAPTER 2
# TOP 10 MOST EXPENSIVE CARS OF 2014

In the next chapter you'll read about the crazy prices that people are prepared to pay for individual machines with extraordinary histories. Four out of five of them are worth over £20m each. Here, however, we've found you the very priciest brand new motors of 2014. Prepare to put your nose up against the metaphorical window of the prestige marque showrooms and drool.

We've not counted different editions of the same make and model, e.g. only one kind of Bugatti Veyron – but they're all still at least a million dollars!

www.unrealautos.com

# 10.

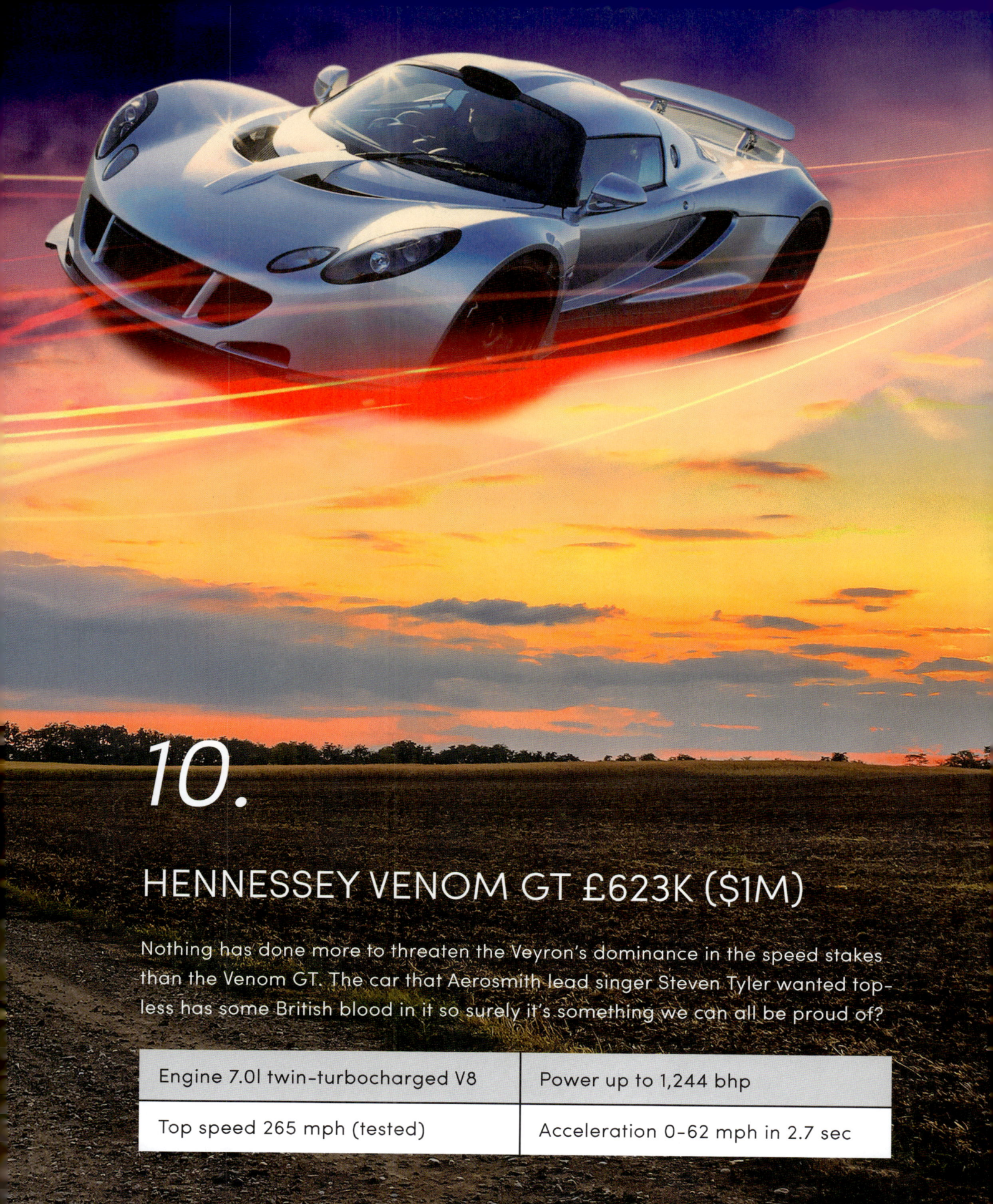

## HENNESSEY VENOM GT £623K ($1M)

Nothing has done more to threaten the Veyron's dominance in the speed stakes than the Venom GT. The car that Aerosmith lead singer Steven Tyler wanted topless has some British blood in it so surely it's something we can all be proud of?

| Engine 7.0l twin-turbocharged V8 | Power up to 1,244 bhp |
| Top speed 265 mph (tested) | Acceleration 0–62 mph in 2.7 sec |

www.unrealautos.com

# 9. MCLAREN P1 £866K ($1.39M)

Calling the new McLaren the P1 is as shameless an attempt to associate it with the F1 as calling the new Jag the F-Type because of the E-Type. Will it live up to the hype though? Like LaFerrari (at number 8) it is a hybrid, and like the F1, it is a mid-engined rear wheel drive beast, so perhaps we should expect great things.

| Engine 3.8l twin-turbocharged V8 | Power 903 bhp |
| --- | --- |
| Top speed 217 mph | Acceleration 0-62 mph in 2.9 sec |

## 8.
# FERRARI F70 LAFERRARI £900K ($1.45M)

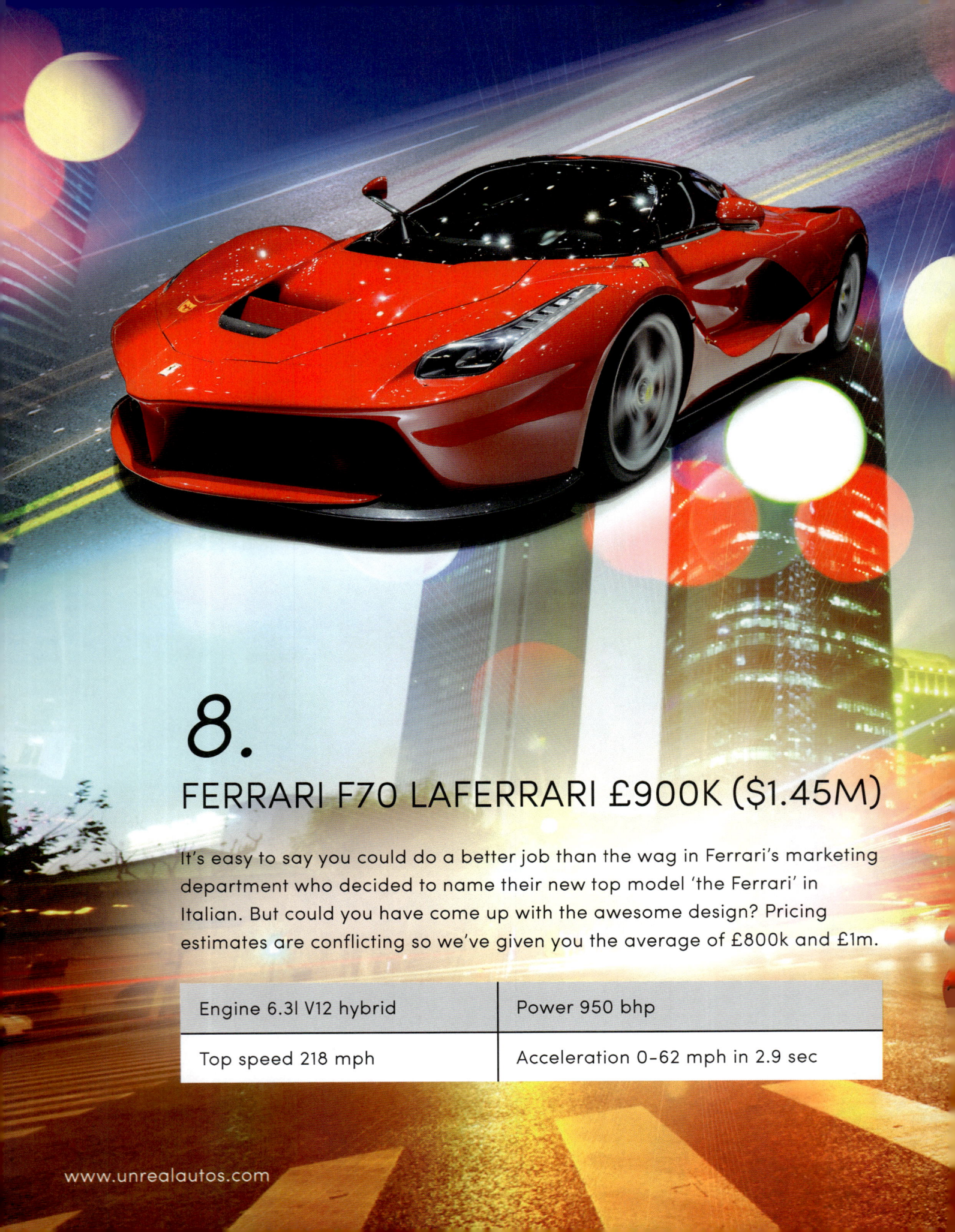

It's easy to say you could do a better job than the wag in Ferrari's marketing department who decided to name their new top model 'the Ferrari' in Italian. But could you have come up with the awesome design? Pricing estimates are conflicting so we've given you the average of £800k and £1m.

| Engine 6.3l V12 hybrid | Power 950 bhp |
| --- | --- |
| Top speed 218 mph | Acceleration 0-62 mph in 2.9 sec |

www.unrealautos.com

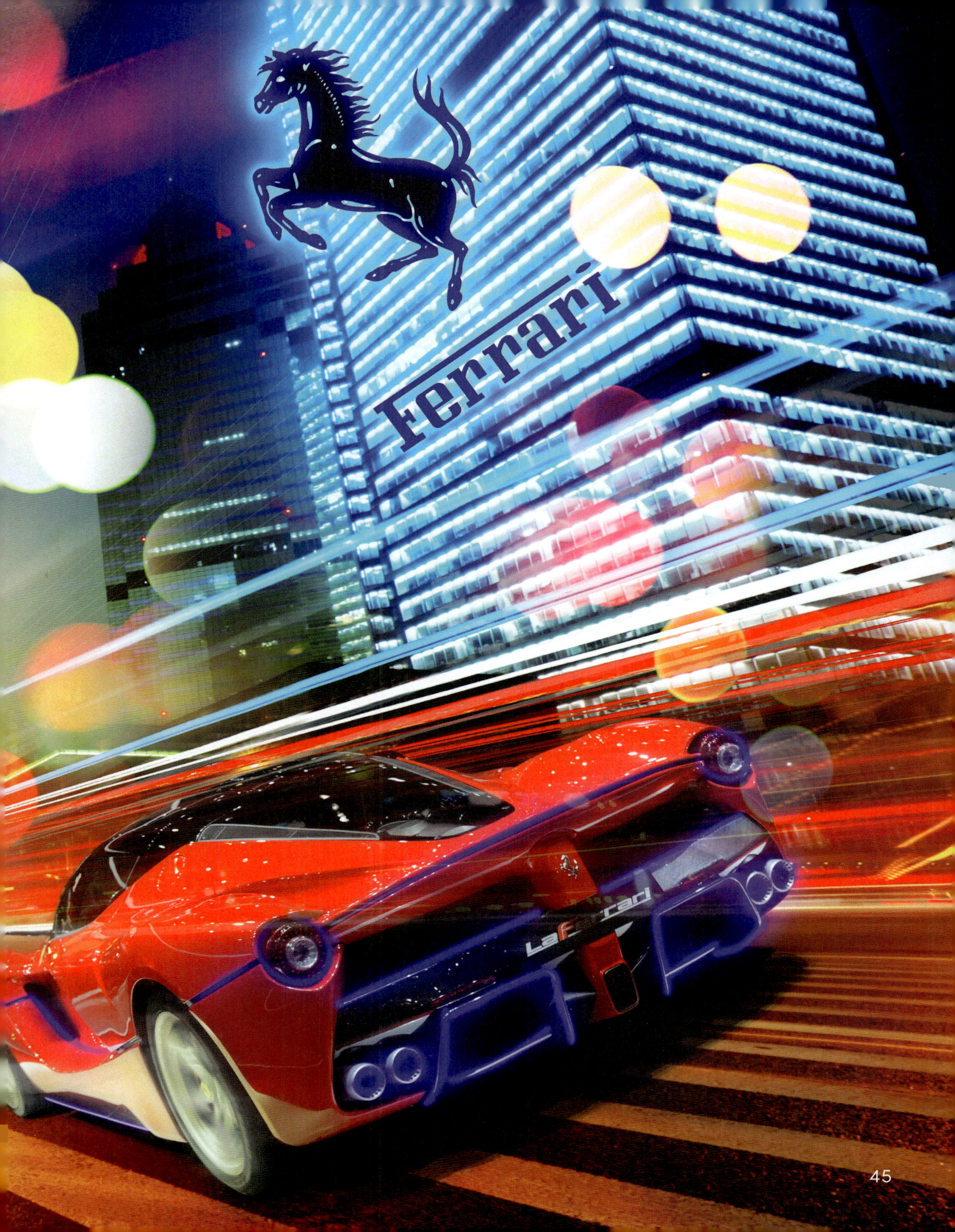
Ferrari
LaFerrari

# 7.
## PAGANI HUAYRA £1.03M ($1.65M)

The Huayra might be junior to the Zonda Revolucion in the price tag stakes (despite a big hike this year) but it's no slouch when the rubber hits the road. TG fans won't need reminding that this car still holds the top spot in the Stig's Power Lap table with a time of 1 minute 13.8 seconds.

| Engine 6.0l bi-turbocharged V12 | Power 720 bhp |
| --- | --- |
| Top speed 230 mph | Acceleration 0-60 mph in 3.3 sec |

www.unrealautos.com

DOWNLOAD THESE PHOTOS AS
DESKTOP WALLPAPERS OR POSTERS
Go to www.unrealautos.com/wallpapers

# 6.
## ZENVO ST-1 £1.12M ($1.8M)

Contrary to some opinion, the ST-1 did not cease production in 2009. In fact it only entered production that year, and with a three per year schedule and 15 total planned, it should still be rolling off the factory into 2014.

| | |
|---|---|
| Engine 7.0l turbo-supercharged V8 | Power 1104 hp (non-US configuration) |
| Top speed 233 mph | Acceleration 0-62 mph in 3.0 sec |

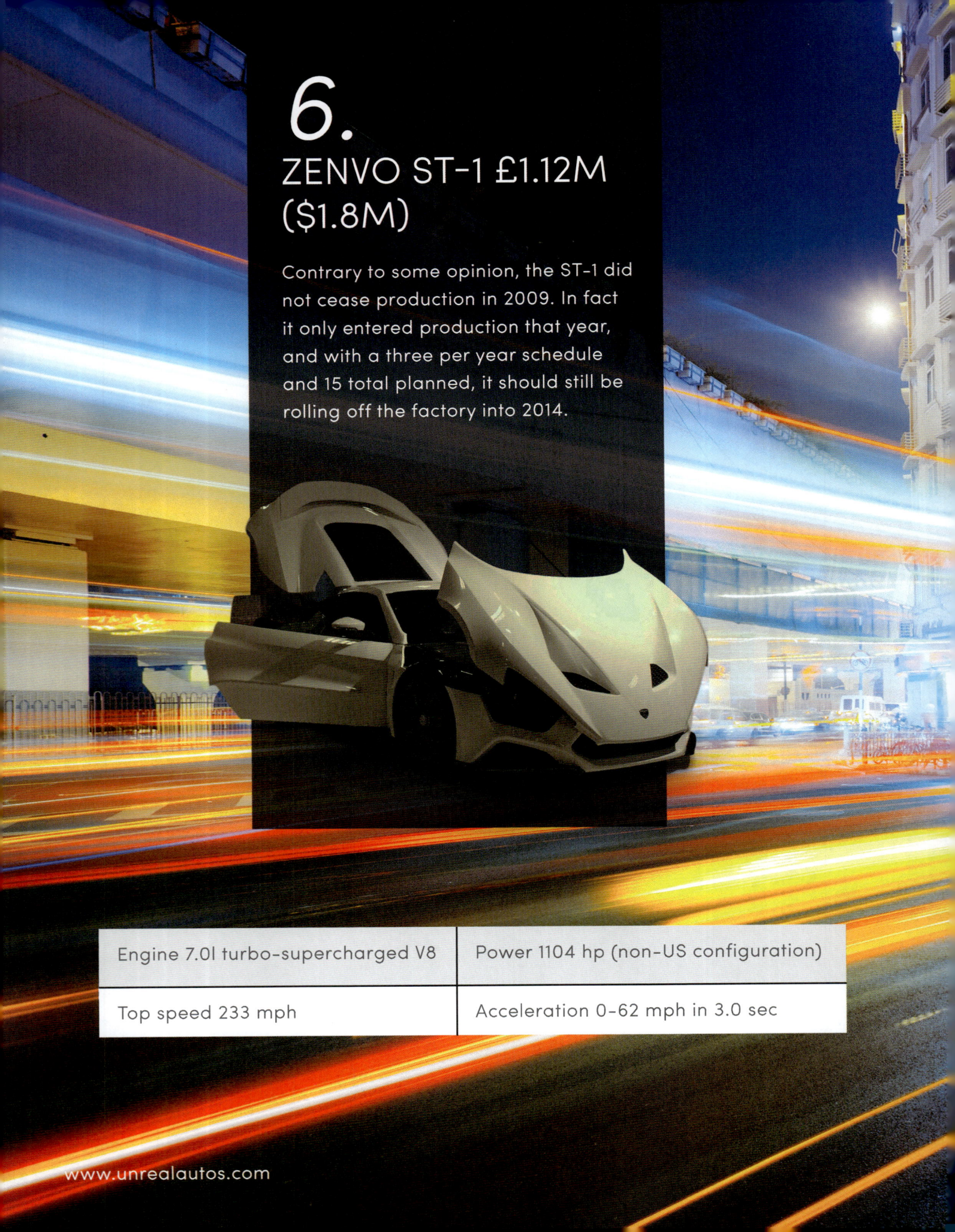

www.unrealautos.com

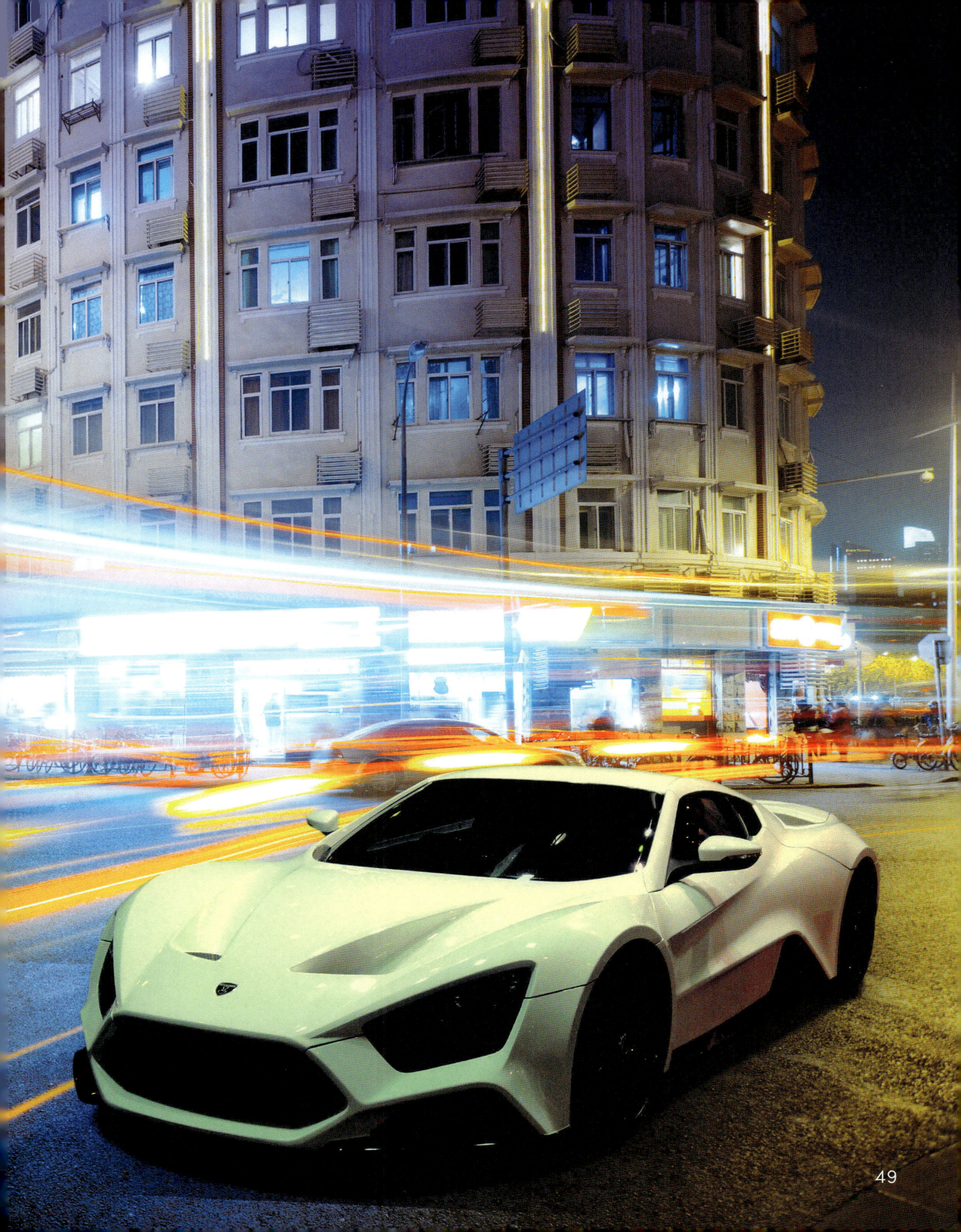

www.unrealautos.com

# 5.

## BUGATTI VEYRON 16.4 GRAND SPORT VITESSE JEAN-PIERRE WIMILLE EDITION £2.1M ($3.37M)

You may have been expecting the SS or Super Sport but we give you the Jean-Pierre Wimille Edition, notable for its especially high price tag, even for a Bugatti. Of course, if VW weren't strategically selling the Veyron at a loss, the true price tag would make this our no.1 expensive car – at around $8.8m each.

| Engine 8.0l W16 | Power 1200 hp |
| --- | --- |
| Top speed 254 mph – with the top down! | Acceleration 0–62 mph in 2.6 sec |

www.unrealautos.com

## 4.
### W MOTORS' LYKAN HYPERSPORT £2.12M ($3.4M)

If there's a joker in the pack then this is it. Firstly, what kind of a car comes out of Lebanon? Secondly, real gemstones in the headlights that the buyer can customise? Yes, it uses titanium LED blades with 420 diamonds. O---kay.

| Engine 3.7l flat-6 | Power 750 hp |
|---|---|
| Top speed 240 mph | Acceleration 0-62 mph in 2.8 sec |

# 3.
## PAGANI ZONDA REVOLUCION
## £2.3M ($3.7M)

One of the great achievements of Pagani has been how its Zonda dates back over a decade but still holds its own against much newer competition. The Spanish word Revolucion is a cheeky development of Pagani's R Evolution, and is the final incarnation of the Zonda – allegedly.

| Engine 6.0l V12    | Power 800 hp                      |
|--------------------|-----------------------------------|
| Top speed 218 mph  | Acceleration 0–62 mph in 2.6 sec  |

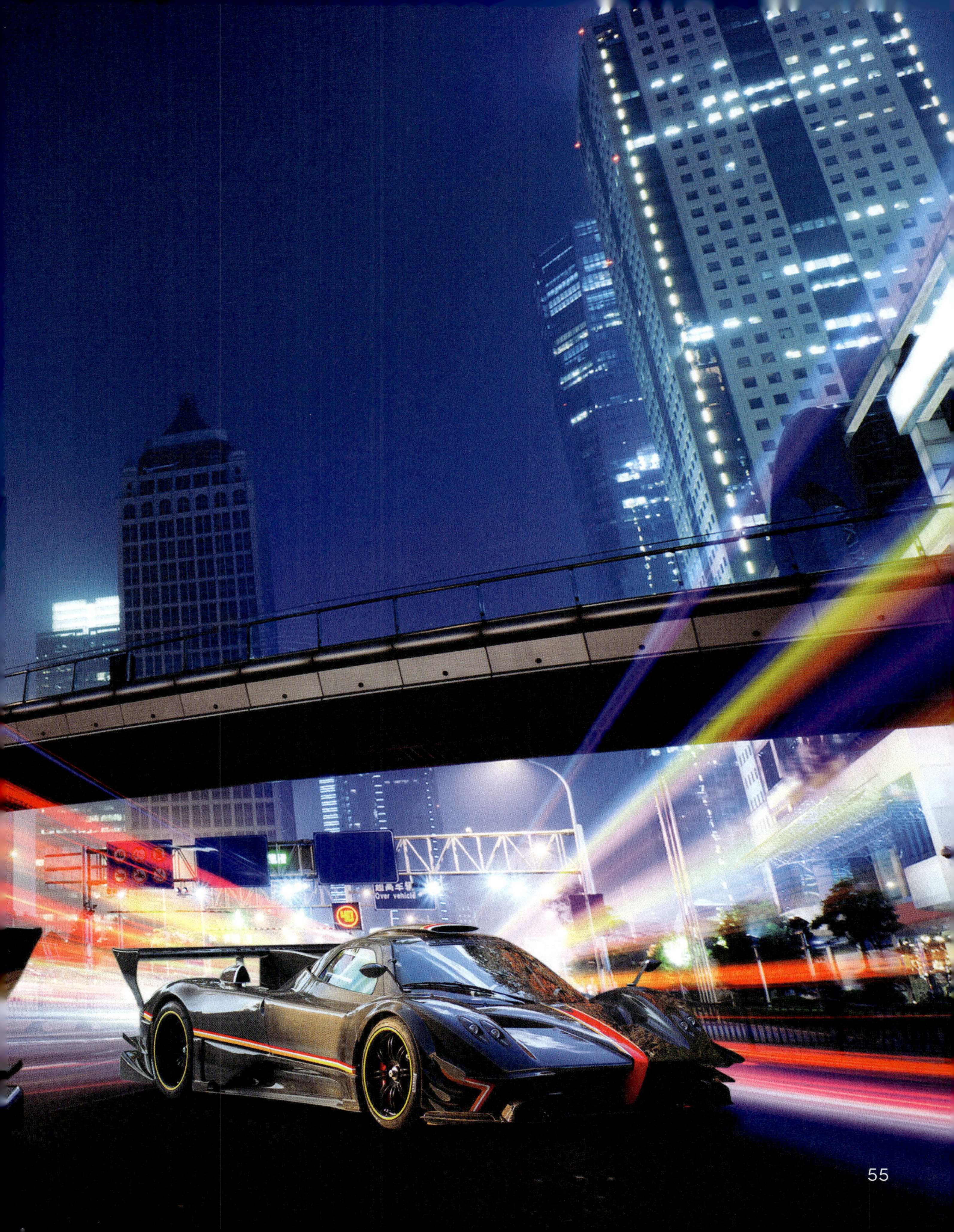
Over vehicle

## 2.
### LAMBORGHINI VENENO
### £2.54M ($4.1M)

No surprise to see the Veneno high in our Top 10. Lambo's dearest street-legal production car has apparently just achieved its first real customer delivery. If you imagine an Aventador putting on the mask in Jim Carrey's eponymous film, you get Lamborghini's 50th anniversary present to just 3 potential owners.

| Engine 6.5l V12 | Power 740 hp |
|---|---|
| Top speed 221 mph | Acceleration 0-60 mph in 2.8 sec |

www.unrealautos.com

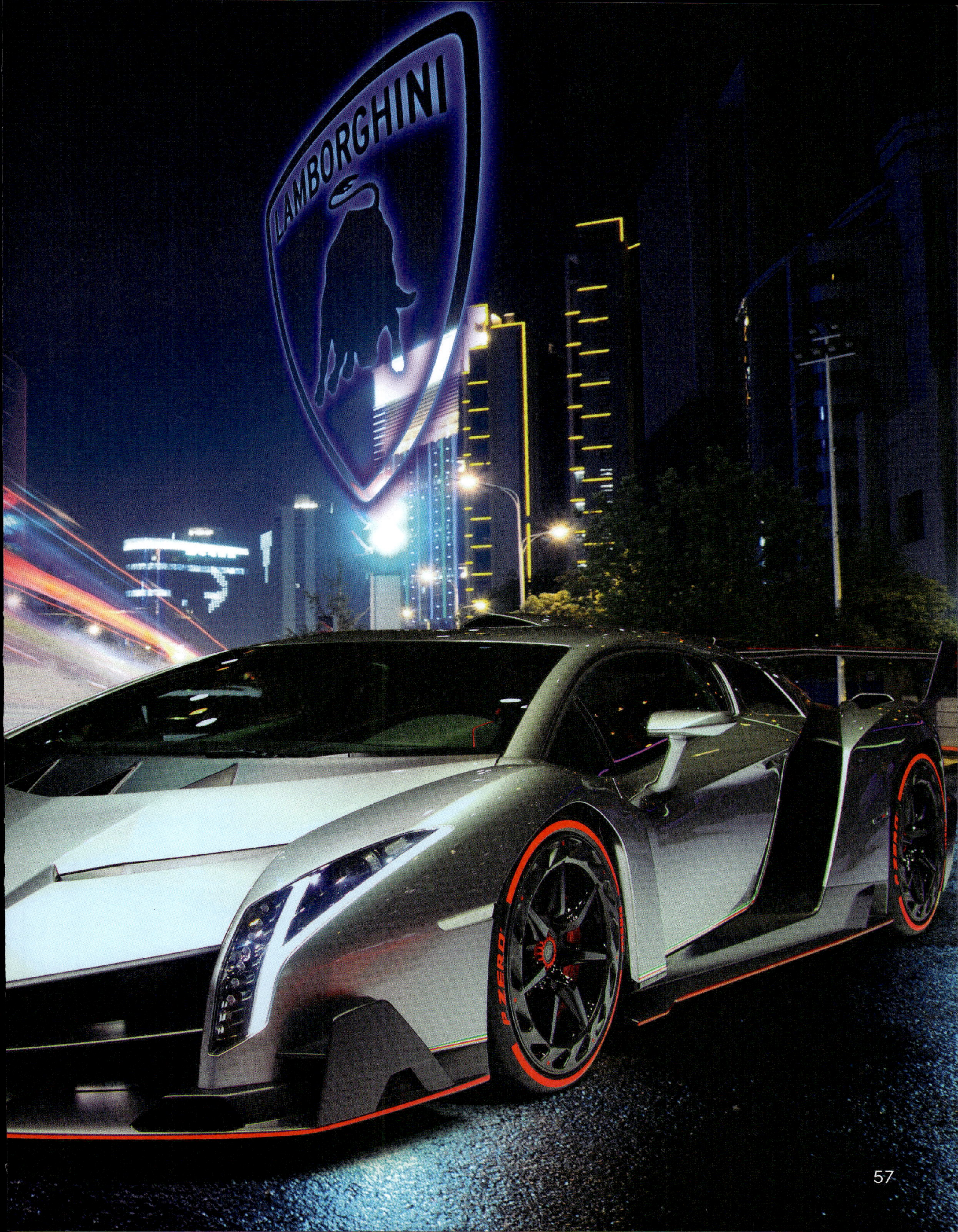
LAMBORGHINI
P ZERO

# 1.
## KOENIGSEGG AGERA S
## £2.6M ($4.2M)

Yes, that's right, an Agera tops our list, which is perhaps the biggest surprise of all. The key to it is that 'S' as the Agera R is a whole $2.5m cheaper. Koenigsegg's new flagship hypercar sold for the eye-watering sum above at a private launch event in Singapore.

Engine:
5.0l twin-turbo-supercharged V8

Power:
1040 hp

Top speed:
249 mph

Acceleration:
0-62 mph in 2.9 sec

www.unrealautos.com

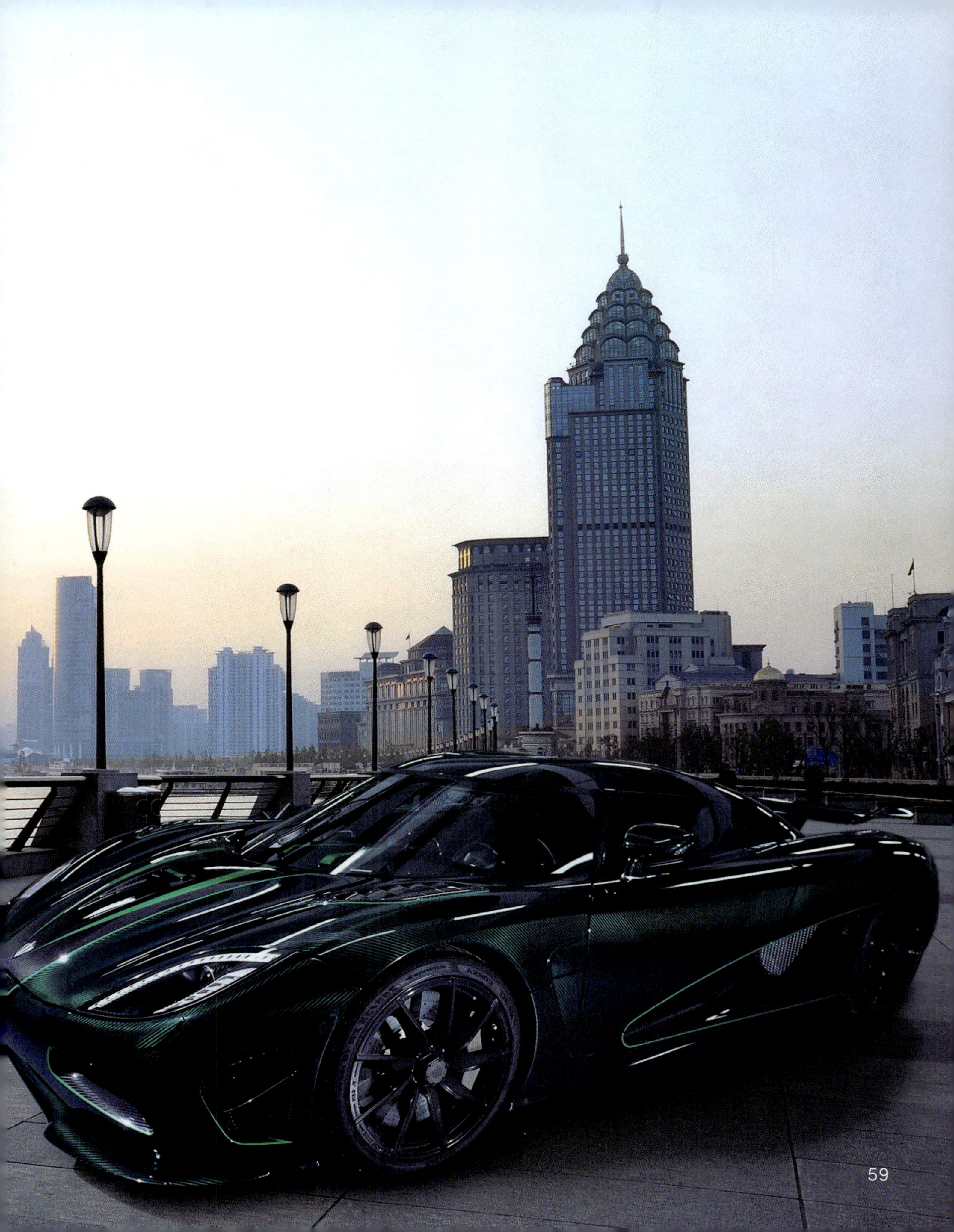

www.unrealautos.com

## Did you Know?
There are eight official State limousines operated for the British Royal Family, comprised of three Rolls-Royces, two Bentleys and three Daimlers. State cars are painted in royal claret livery and need no licence plates in the UK.

www.unrealautos.com

As covers of shimmering silk
Are blown from the roof
Oceans of scarlet steel
Are revealed from beneath

A raging bull
A spoiler, a flash of chrome exhaust
And then a spark

From key to spark to cylinder
A lion – nay two
Must be trapped inside
Unable to get out
Or vent any feeling
But through the rubber to the road

As lightning is to thunder
Is this legend to the wind

CHAPTER 3
# THE TOP 5 MOST VALUABLE CARS IN THE WORLD

Here's Unreal Auto's rundown of the top 5 most valuable individual machines in the world. We're including anything, no matter how old, but do check out our separate Top 10 Most Expensive Cars article for the list of current brand new motors on sale.

Here though we've taken into account actual auction sale prices but also cars which have an estimated worth in 2014 money, even if they haven't changed hands for a very long time. The final figures and relative positions are subject to fierce debate.

www.unrealautos.com

# 5.
## 1936 BUGATTI TYPE 57SC ATLANTIC

Due to the secretive nature of the transaction, the best estimate for the final price, was US$30-40m. That's a lot of Dacia Sanderos, Mr May.

The jury's still out on whether this ahead-of-its-time pre-war speed machine is beautiful, or resembles a labrador's head. Either way though, only two or three have survived, and one was even controversially reconstructed from the remains of a collision that claimed the lives of its occupants.

www.unrealautos.com

# 4.

## STIRLING MOSS' 1962 FERRARI 250 GTO

Beginning a Moss theme in this chapter, we have the first of our cars to be backed up with an actual sale price. Just last year, another 250 GTO fetched £22m (US$35m) at auction.

Although built for Moss, injury prevented him from driving it in anger. The racer who would take it to Tourist Trophy victory at Goodwood was Innes Ireland.

www.unrealautos.com

# 3.
## STIRLING MOSS' 1955 '722' MERCEDES-BENZ 300 SLR

This is a great car made greater by its association with racing legend Stirling Moss. In 1955 the '722' helped Moss to World Sportscar Championship glory, and broke the Italian monopoly on Mille Miglia winners.

Estimated values for this machine vary, with Moss' own website perhaps optimistically suggesting £40m. More independent sources have put it at £29m (US$47m).

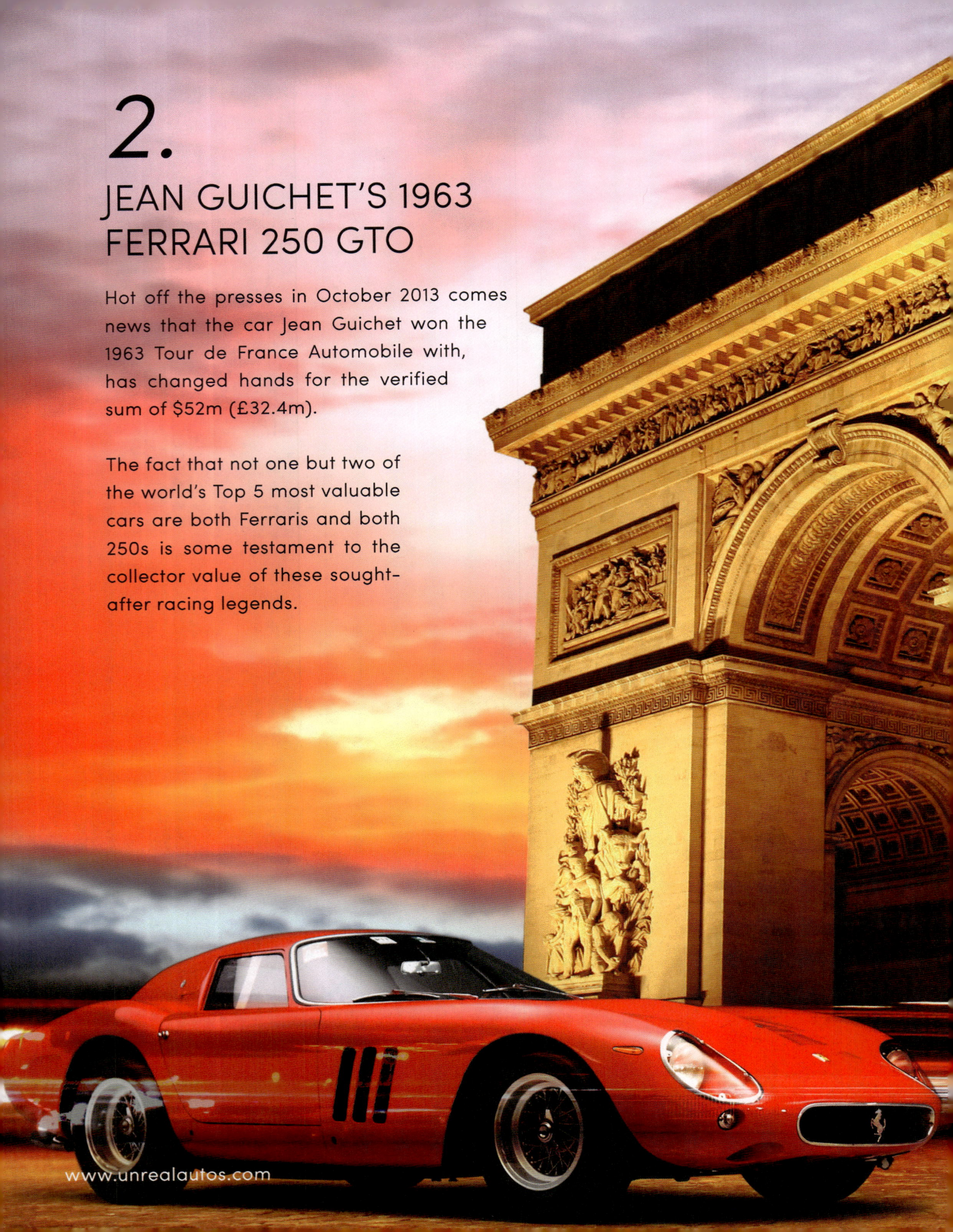

# 2.
## JEAN GUICHET'S 1963 FERRARI 250 GTO

Hot off the presses in October 2013 comes news that the car Jean Guichet won the 1963 Tour de France Automobile with, has changed hands for the verified sum of $52m (£32.4m).

The fact that not one but two of the world's Top 5 most valuable cars are both Ferraris and both 250s is some testament to the collector value of these sought-after racing legends.

www.unrealautos.com

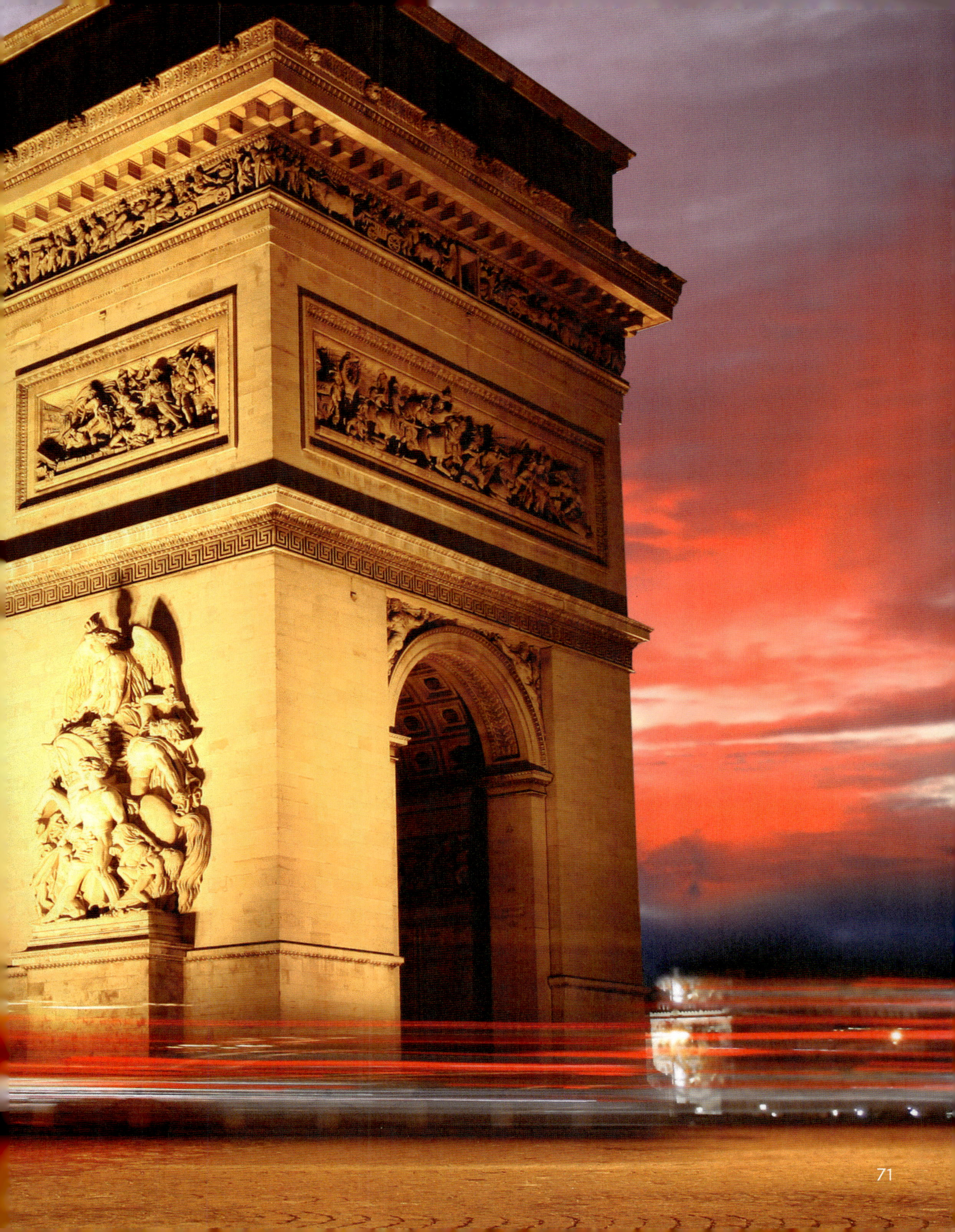

www.unrealautos.com

## 1. 1907 ROLLS ROYCE SILVER GHOST AX201

Coming in at no. 1 we have the ultimate car, if not in original cost, then certainly in current value, were it to be put up for sale. Known to enthusiasts by its UK registration number AX201, it was built as a marketing tool for Rolls Royce in 1907.

VW hinted years ago that it was insured for a sum, which in 2013 money, would be at least $53m (£33m) – that's right, fifty-three million dollars. If you've just made a killing in hedge funds and are looking for a good investment, you'll have to hold your fire though.

The only Silver Ghost to be made with actual silver plating is not likely to come onto the market any time soon. Currently owned by Bentley, it has driven over 500,000 miles around the world and continues to be kept roadworthy. This specific individual car, Chassis no. 60551, did more than anything else to earn RR the independently given sobriquet, 'the best car in the world'.

# WOW!

The biggest-selling single-design car model of all time is the original Type 1 Volkswagen Beetle, which sold 21.5 million units 1938-2003. The Toyota Corolla sold more, but across several different design generations.

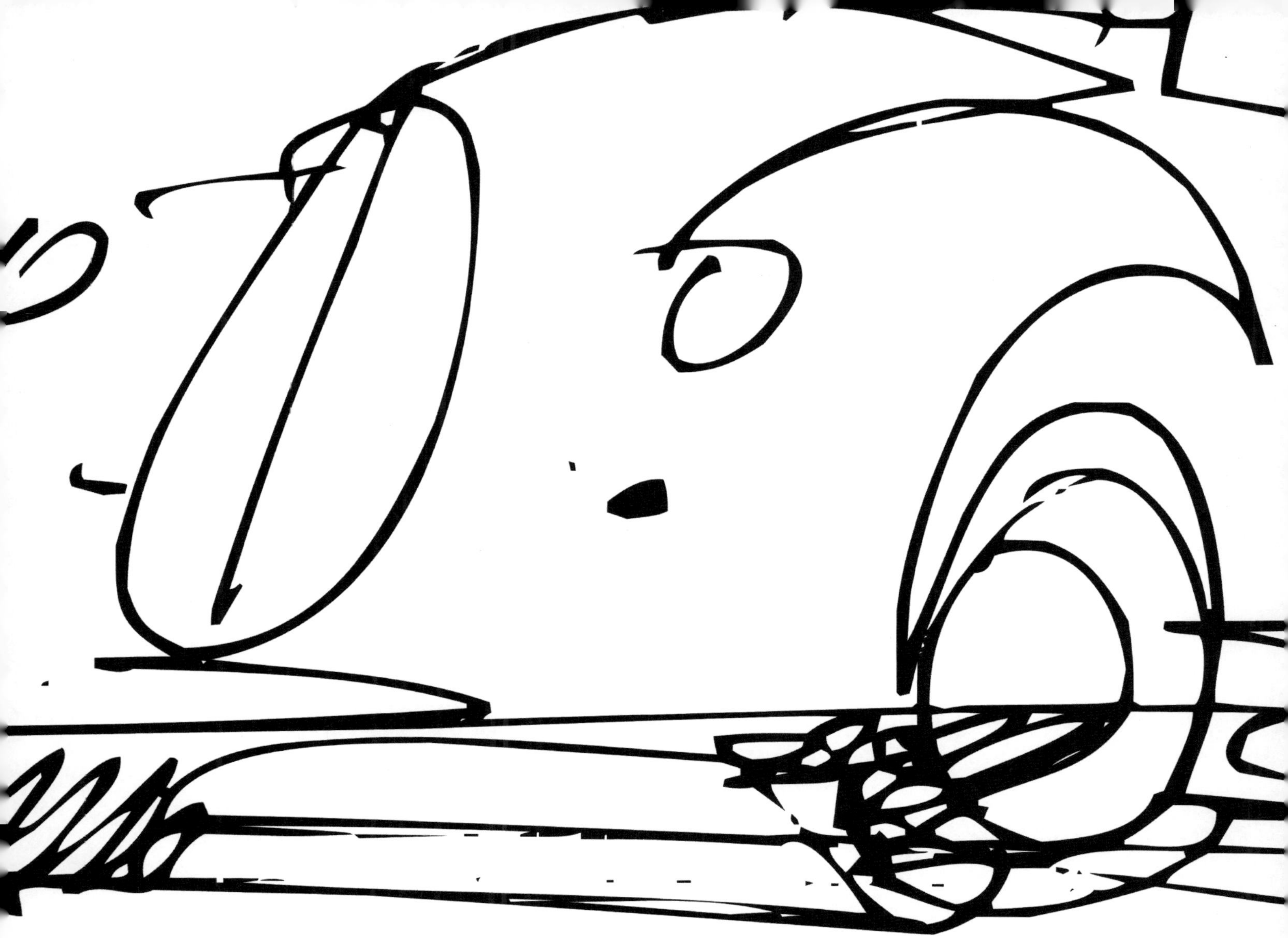

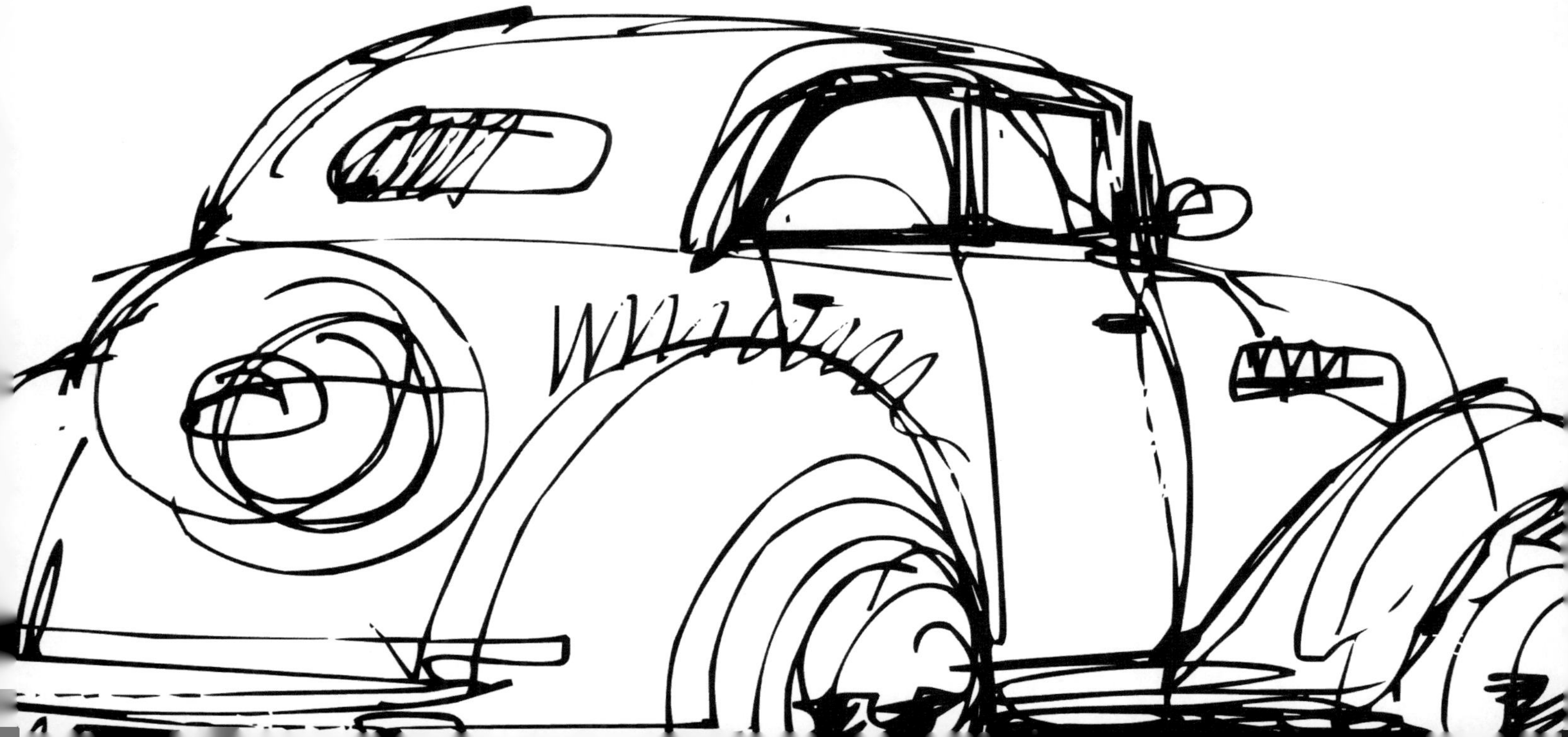

www.unrealautos.com

This guy's having a good time. But did you spot who's driving the Lambo?

How pink is the sky
How long the way ahead
No houses, no cars, no roadside bars
In that moment
The car my sole companion
The heartbeat of its engine
The only sound
Sharing the moment with me
From tunnel to hairpin bend.

# CHAPTER 4
# 10 IMPORTANT MILESTONES IN CAR HISTORY

After Karl Benz built the first Motorwagen in 1885, what next? What were the ten most important safety, performance and car comfort breakthroughs?

Or, to put it another way, what were the first cars to be fitted with various features or to pass important milestones?

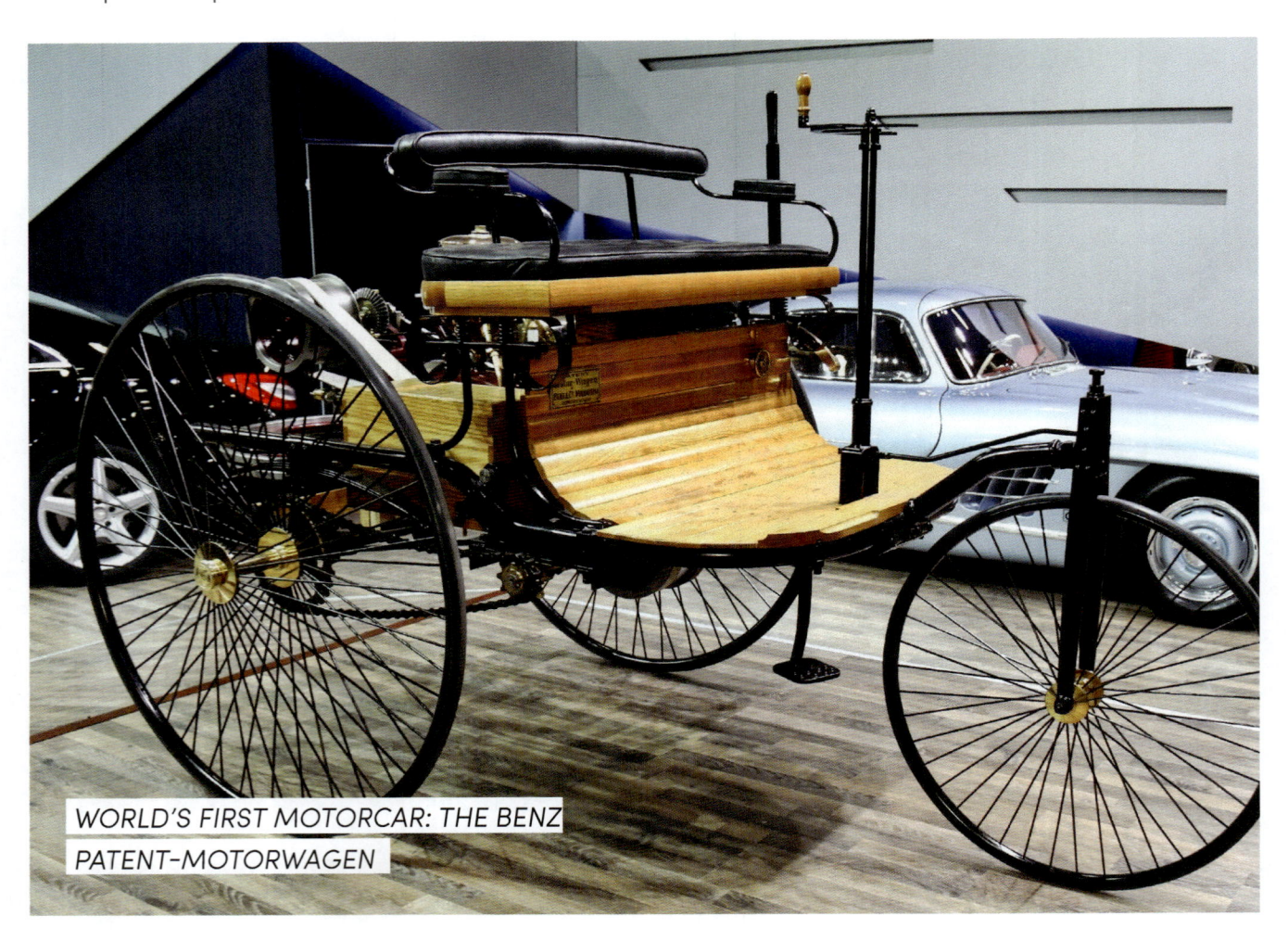

*WORLD'S FIRST MOTORCAR: THE BENZ PATENT-MOTORWAGEN*

# SAFETY

## 1ST CAR WITH ELECTRIC HEADLAMPS (1898)

The Columbia Electric Car of Hartford, Connecticut, was the first motor vehicle to have electric headlights, following the rather unreliable and inconvenient oil and acetylene lamps of earlier automobiles. Think fire hazard.

## 1ST CAR WITH SEAT BELTS (1948)

The Tucker 'Torpedo' '48 of Chicago, Illinois, was the first car to get seat belts plus a number of other safety features that were very far ahead of its time. It even had a third middle headlight that turned in the direction of the steering wheel!

## 1ST CAR WITH CRUMPLE ZONES (1959)

Although patented in 1952, it would be another 7 years before Mercedes-Benz put crumple zone technology into a production car for real. The W111 Heckflosse or Fintail had front and rear zones to absorb crash energy.

## 1ST CAR WITH AIRBAGS (1971-73)

The rise (excuse the pun) of airbags started with Ford's experimental fleet of airbag-enabled cars in 1971. Government-use Chevrolets followed in 1973. The first publicly available passenger car was the 1973 Oldsmobile Toronado.

# PERFORMANCE

## 1ST CAR TO HAVE 4-WHEEL DRIVE (1903)

The 1900 Porsche/Lohner La Toujours Contente had four independent electric hub motors, but the 1903 Dutch Spyker 60 h.p. was the first car to have full-time, mechanical 4WD in the engine and shaft-driven way we are familiar with today.

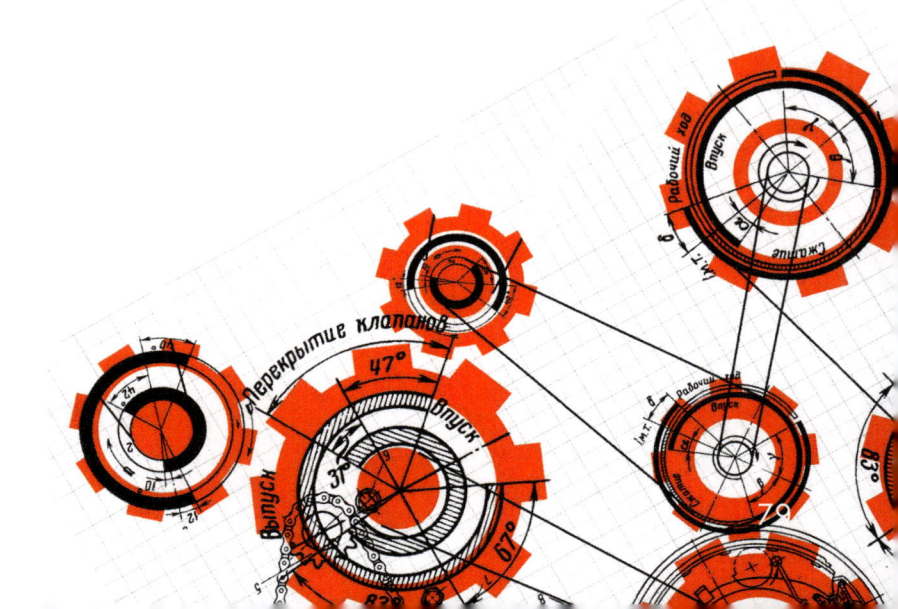

# 1ST CAR TO 100MPH (1904)

For Ostende Automobile Week, Louis Rigolly drove his 15-litre (yes fifteen!) Gobron-Brillié at an average speed of 103.56 mph over a kilometre. Such speeds were unheard of until this point.

# 1ST CAR TO 200MPH (1927)

The first road-legal, unmodified, non-racing, production car to break this barrier was the Ferrari F40 in 1987. The Dodge Charger Daytona and Ford GT-40 came earlier and managed 200, but only in their one-off, modified, racing forms. The 1978 Mercedes-Benz C111 prototype never made it into mass production.

However, the first car of any kind to 200 mph was the Sunbeam 1000 hp Mystery, driven by Henry Segrave to 203 mph on 29 March 1927.

# COMFORT

## 1ST CAR WITH PNEUMATIC TYRES (1895)

Peugeot started fitting solid rubber tyres to cars in 1892 with their Type 4, but inflated Michelin rubber tyres came on their 1895 L'Eclair model. However, they didn't manage to finish the Paris-Bordeaux-Paris race with it.

## 1ST CAR WITH A ROOF (1899)

The world's first saloon came in 1899 with the Renault Voiturette B. As top-heavy as a top hat, and surprisingly similar looking, we can only assume those 19th century motorists weren't trying to send the back end out around corners.

## 1ST CAR WITH FULLY AUTOMATIC TRANSMISSION (1940)

After semi-automatic beginnings in 1937-38 with Oldsmobile and Buick models, the first car to do away with the clutch pedal altogether was the Hydramatic Oldsmobile 1940 model.

*THE 1987 FERRARI F40 WAS THE FIRST ROAD LEGAL PRODUCTION CAR TO BREAK THE 200MPH BARRIER*

www.unrealautos.com

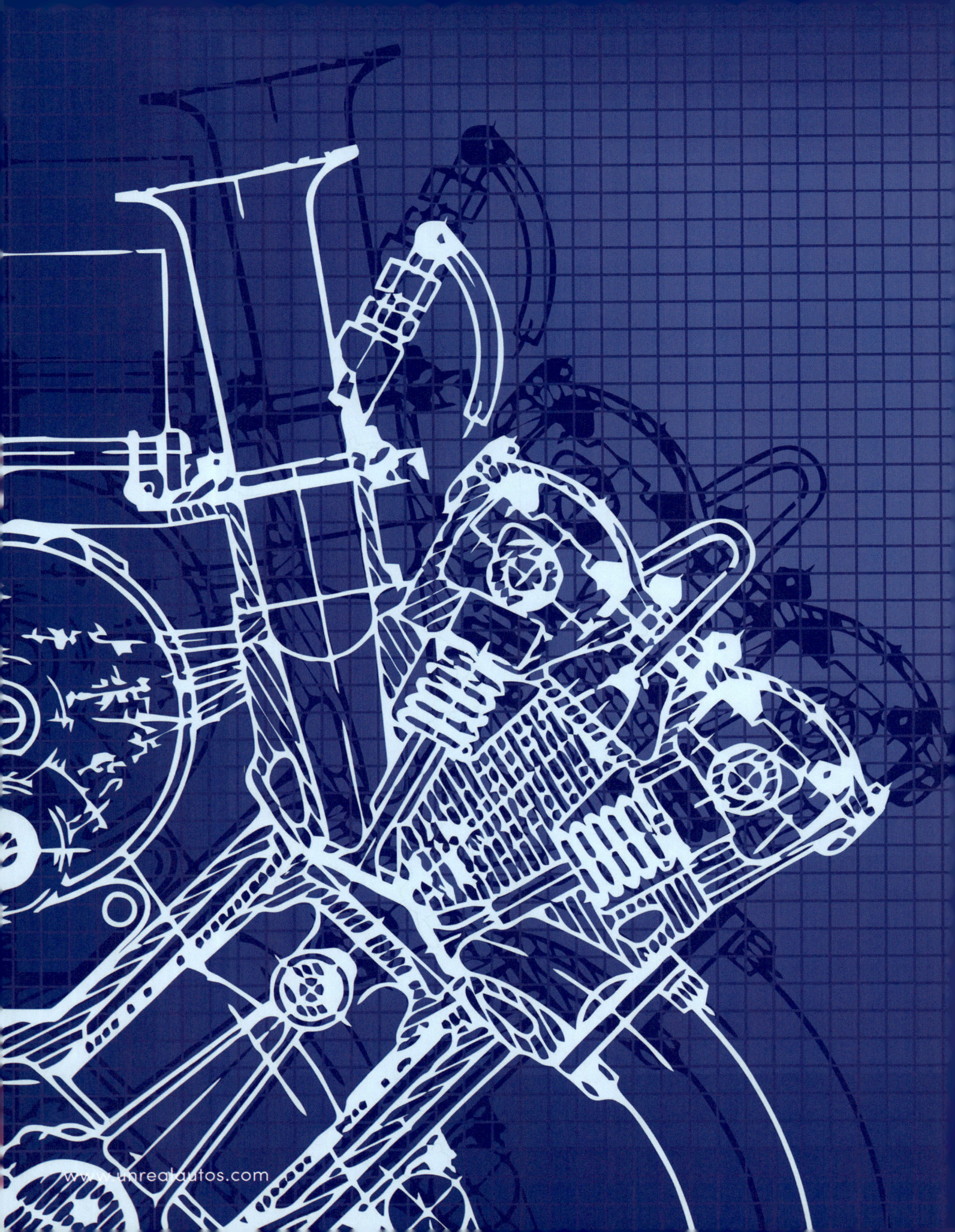

# Double de-clutching

Some readers may remember that early cars – and some large commercial vehicles today – had to change gear by engaging the clutch pedal and moving the stick into Neutral, releasing the pedal, and then re-engaging the pedal to go from neutral to the next gear with the stick. What a hassle!

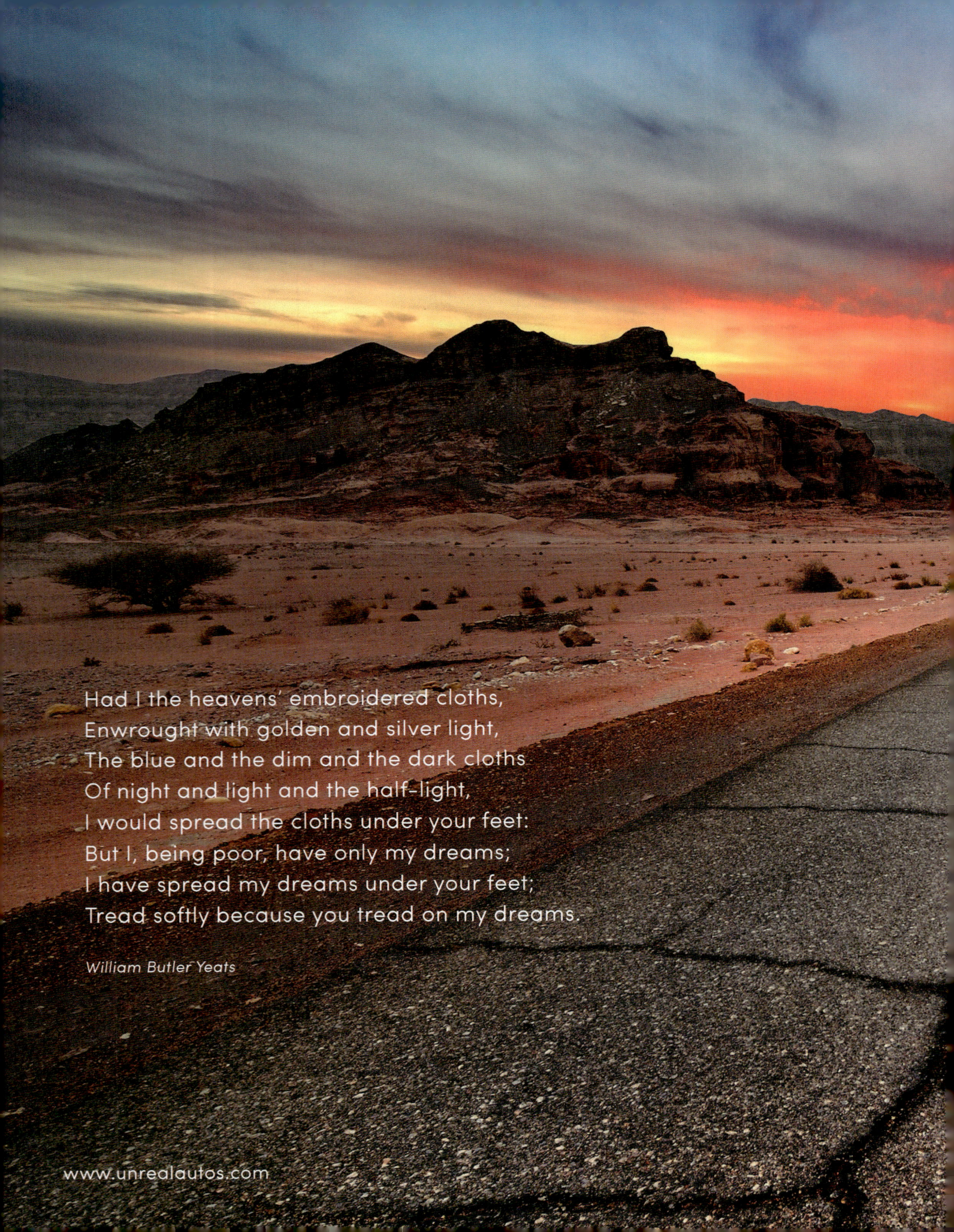

Had I the heavens' embroidered cloths,
Enwrought with golden and silver light,
The blue and the dim and the dark cloths
Of night and light and the half-light,
I would spread the cloths under your feet:
But I, being poor, have only my dreams;
I have spread my dreams under your feet;
Tread softly because you tread on my dreams.

*William Butler Yeats*

www.unrealautos.com

Into the desert
of the future....

# CHAPTER 5
# THE WORLD'S COOLEST CONCEPT CARS

This isn't the good, the bad and the ugly. This is your reliable run-down of the cool, the cooler, and the downright deep-frozen.

Poster cars to make your mouth water are coming in all kinds of flavours. Check out these delectable cool concepts from across the board and prepare to be stunned.

www.unrealautos.com

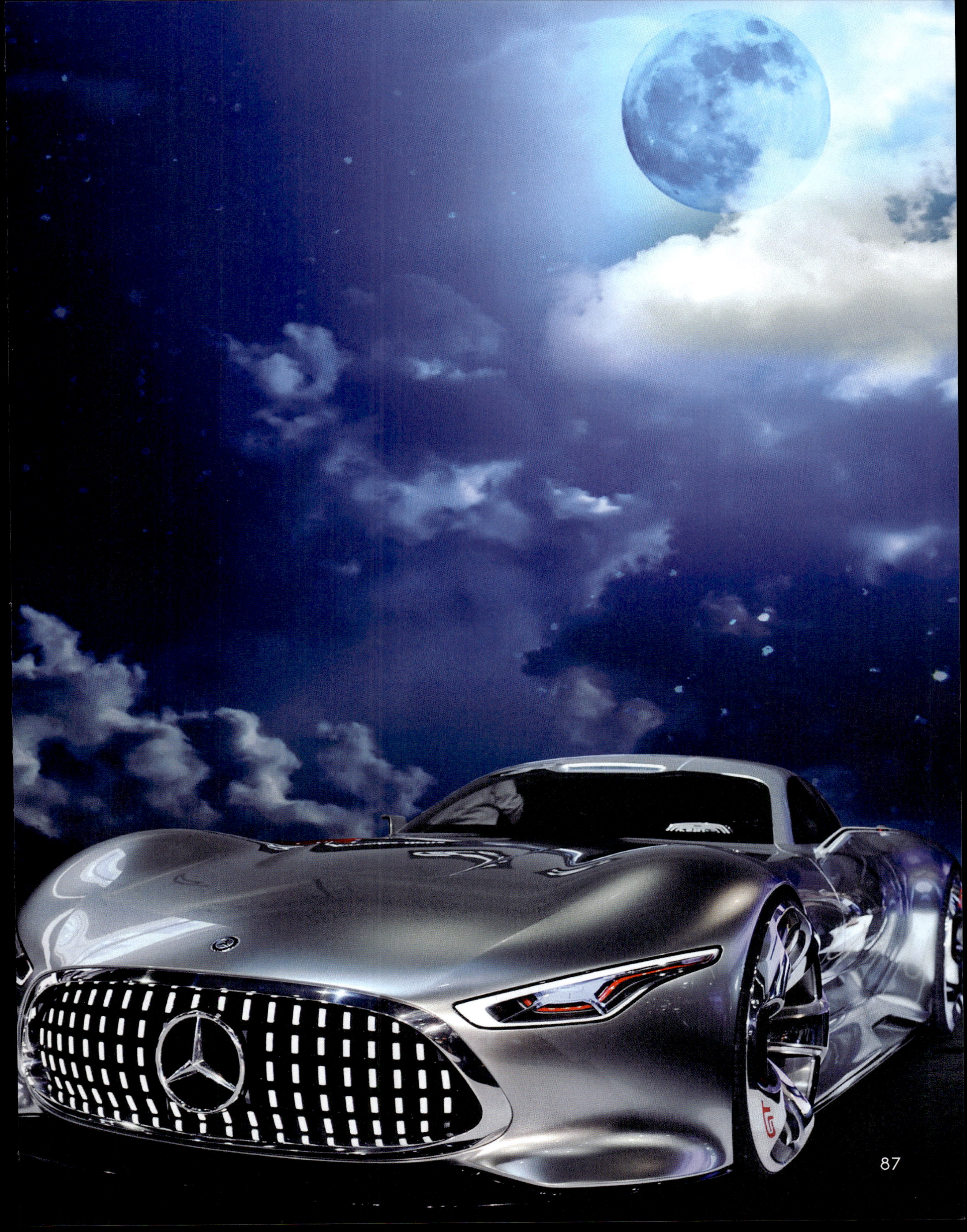

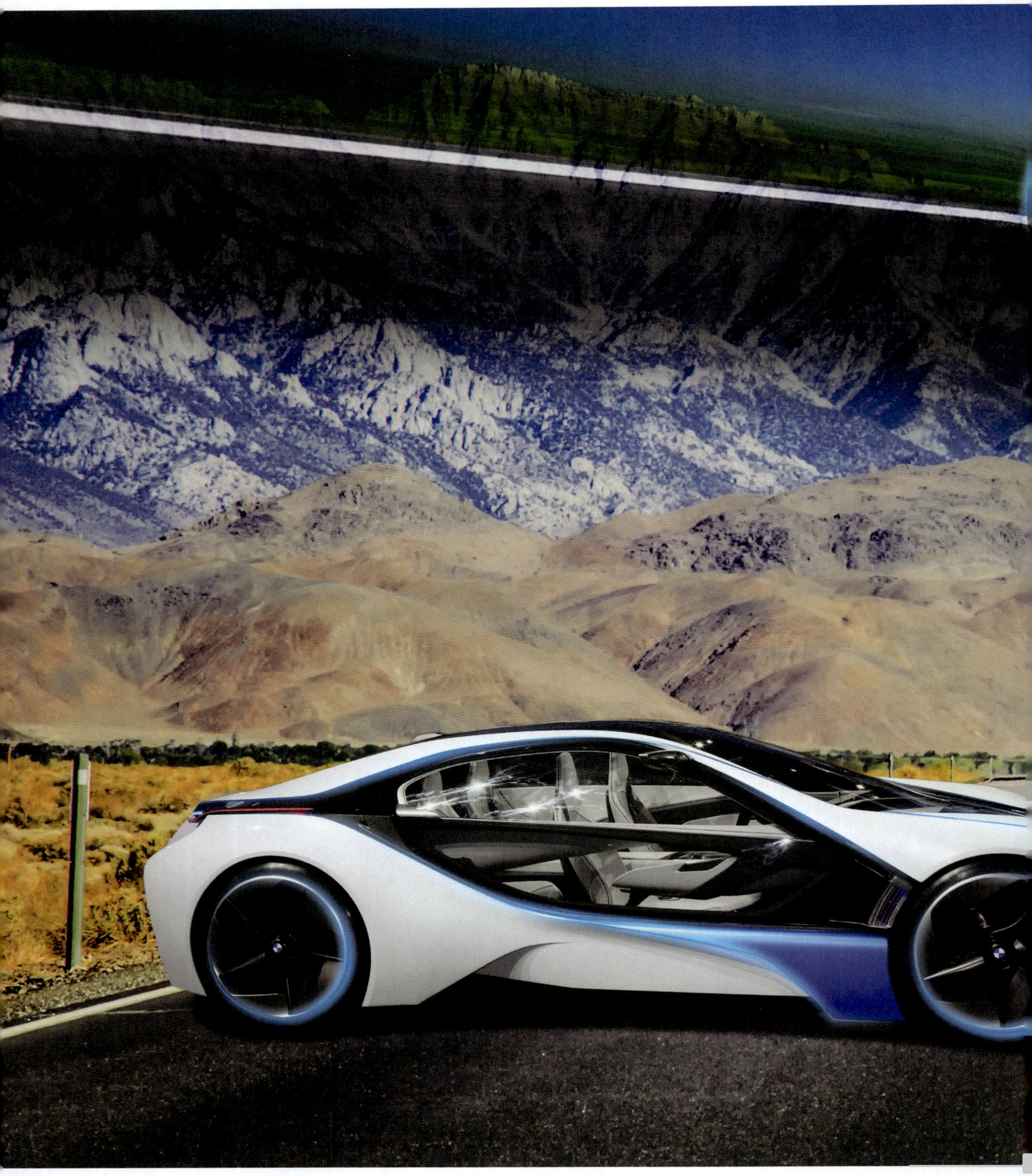

# 10.

## BMW VISION EFFICIENTDYNAMICS (2009)

Any
car that
has a blue-illuminated
radiator grille has to get votes in the
cool stakes. Apart from being highly economical
thanks to its ActiveHybrid technology, the Vision concept has high
wing mirrors for that edgy touch.

www.unrealautos.com

## 9.
### LARAKI EPITOME (2013)

As we come to this futuristic and manly motor, the temperature has, pretty much, become sub-zero. You may not know the Laraki name, and guess what, it's Moroccan, but don't be fooled. It's got Mercedes-Benz, Lamborghini and up to 1,750 hp inside it.

www.unrealautos.com

# 8.
## FERRARI XEZRI (2011)

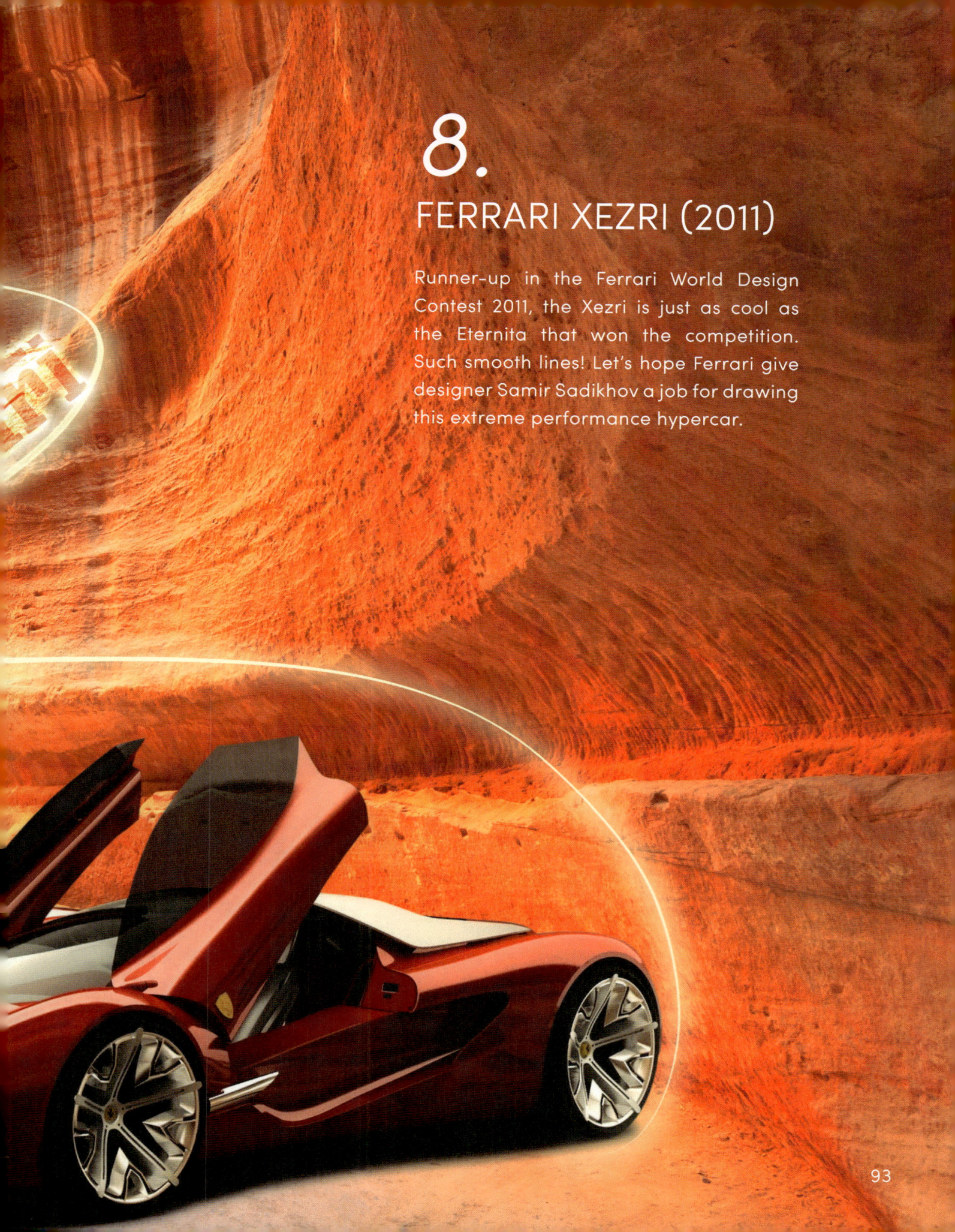

Runner-up in the Ferrari World Design Contest 2011, the Xezri is just as cool as the Eternita that won the competition. Such smooth lines! Let's hope Ferrari give designer Samir Sadikhov a job for drawing this extreme performance hypercar.

www.unrealautos.com

# 7.

## MERCEDES-BENZ SILVER ARROW (2011)

Nothing about this otherworldly design is boring or predictable. Running on omni-directional roller tracks instead of conventional wheels, don't expect this in your local dealership any time soon. Cool ... cool ... cool!

# 6.

## MERCEDES-BENZ BIOME (2010)

Made from a lab-grown material called BioFibre, this vehicle is intended to emit no gas other than oxygen and should grow to the customer's requirements. We kid you not – although it's just possible that Mercedes are describing the dream rather than their ability.

www.unrealautos.com

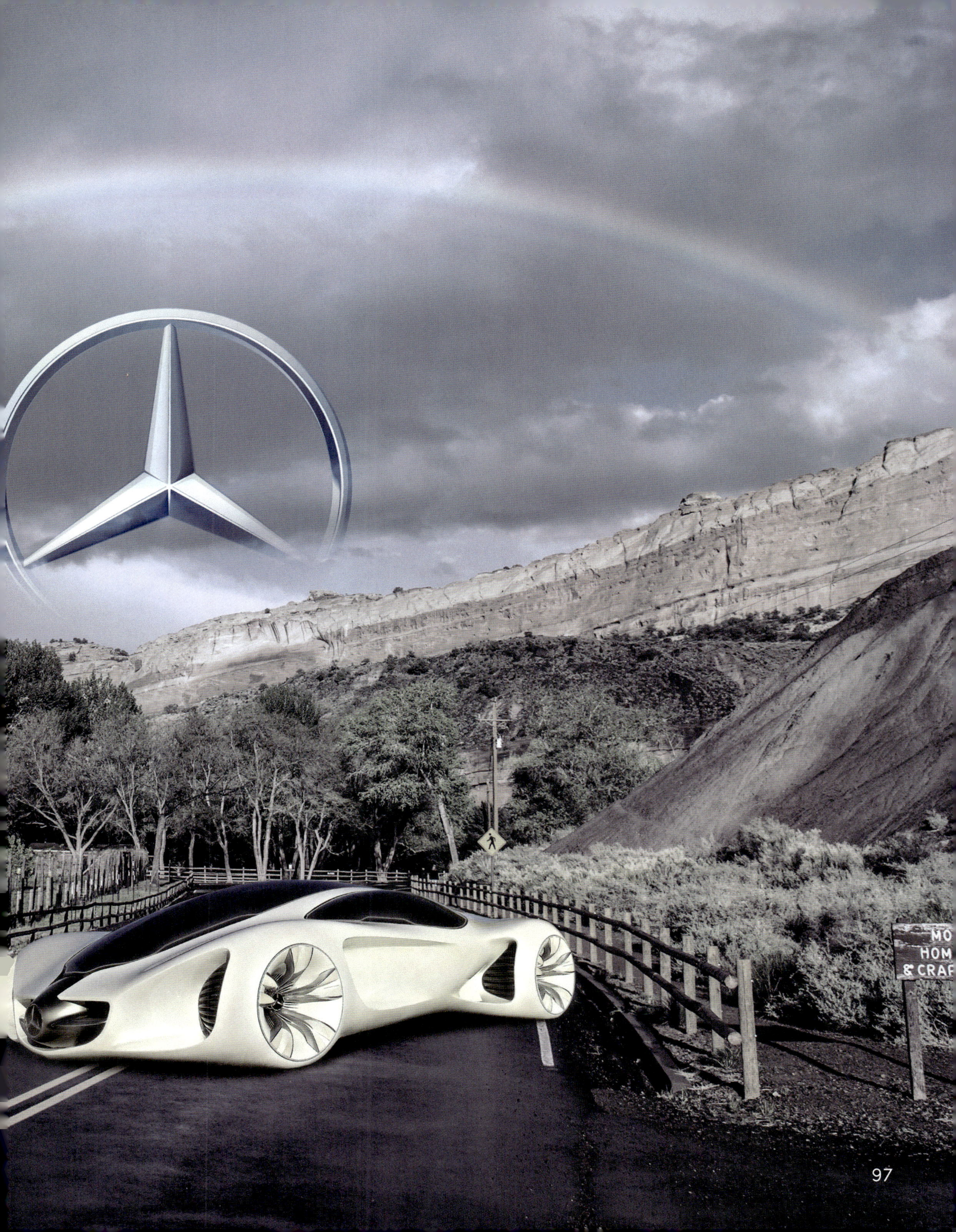
MO
HOM
& CRAF

www.unrealautos.com

# 5.
## JAGUAR C-X75 (2010)

Jaguar cancelled further development of this little artwork in 2012. With a price of around £800,000, it fell victim to the credit crunch. Still, at least we can enjoy the smooth lines of its Lamborghini-like front end and F-Type-like rear. Even the spec reads like the manual for a jet plane. Gas turbines? Really? Originally conceived as the heir to the XJ220, fear not. Both the power-train and the exterior design are set to see use in future Jaguars. Roll on tomorrow!

# 4.

## MASERATI BIRDCAGE 75TH (2005)

Look at this exquisitely sculpted carbon chassis concept. The documentary telling the story of its creation was even called Sleek Dreams. With an all-in-one canopy, instead of doors and hinges to spoil its curves, you could almost be a pilot in a fighter jet. Pity they haven't put it into production.

www.unrealautos.com

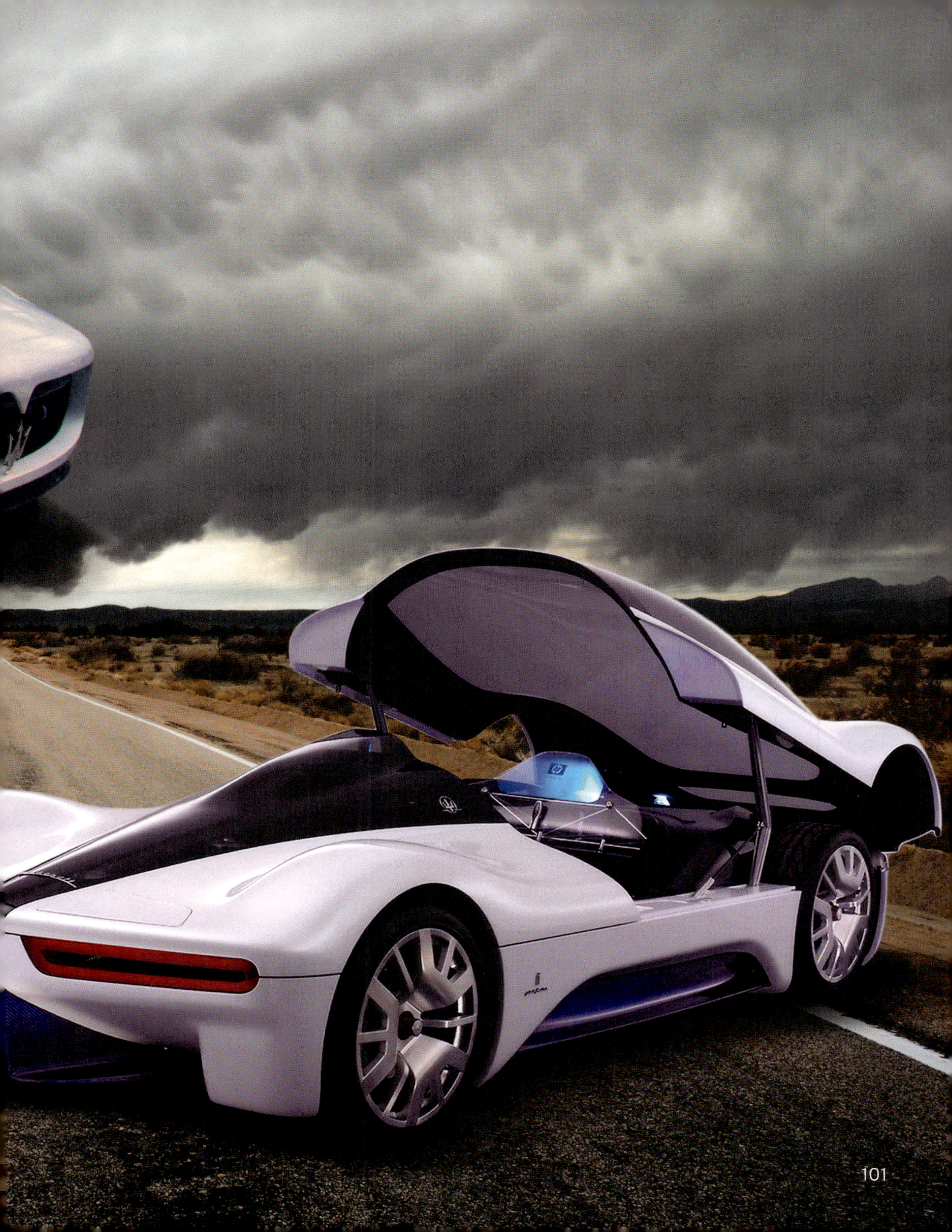

## 3. ASTON MARTIN CC100 (2013)

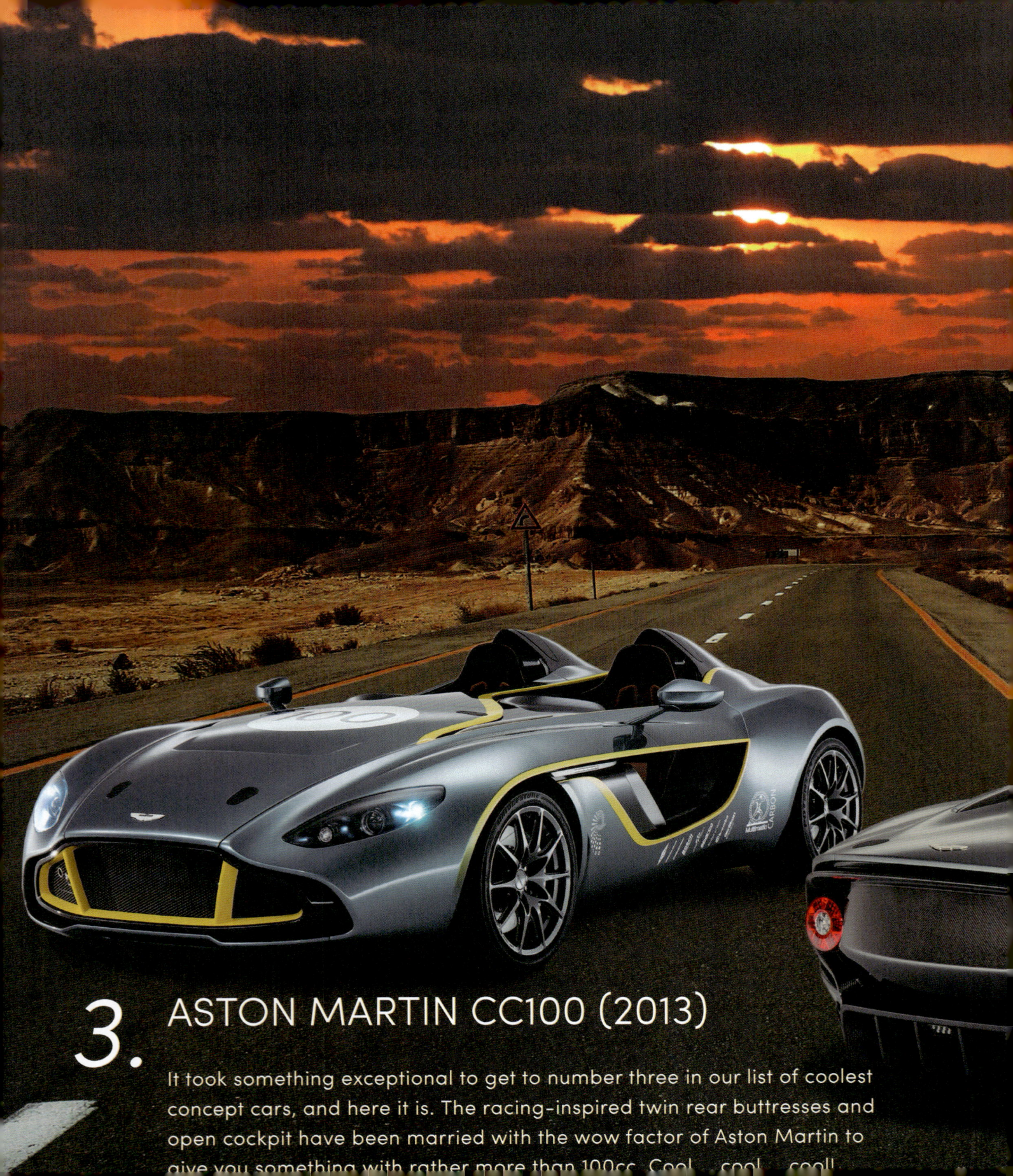

It took something exceptional to get to number three in our list of coolest concept cars, and here it is. The racing-inspired twin rear buttresses and open cockpit have been married with the wow factor of Aston Martin to give you something with rather more than 100cc. Cool... cool... cool!

ASTON MARTIN

www.unrealautos.com

# 2.
## MERCEDES-BENZ VISION GT (2013)

Conceived for the no-holds-barred world of console game Gran Turismo 6, Merc's futuristic feather-light concept features an aluminium space-frame chassis and no fewer than eight exhaust outlets. You could shave yourself in its mirror-like body whilst admiring its 1950s 300SL-inspired grille.

DOWNLOAD THESE PHOTOS AS
DESKTOP WALLPAPERS OR POSTERS
Go to www.unrealautos.com/wallpapers

# 1.
## MORGAN EVA GT (2010)

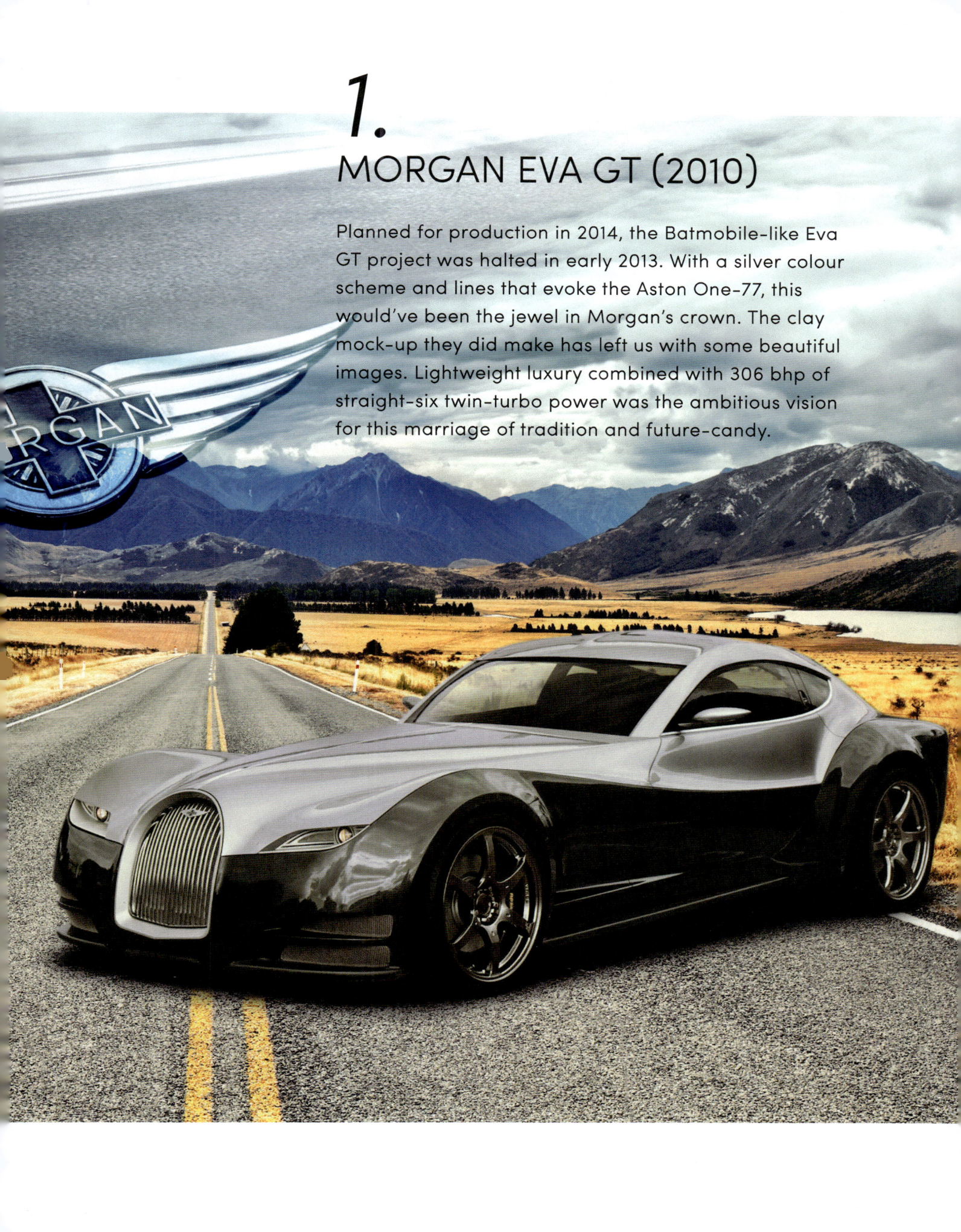

Planned for production in 2014, the Batmobile-like Eva GT project was halted in early 2013. With a silver colour scheme and lines that evoke the Aston One-77, this would've been the jewel in Morgan's crown. The clay mock-up they did make has left us with some beautiful images. Lightweight luxury combined with 306 bhp of straight-six twin-turbo power was the ambitious vision for this marriage of tradition and future-candy.

www.unrealautos.com

# Piles o' scrap

The number of cars scrapped in the UK in 2011 was 1,220,873, up from 995,496 in 2006. In 2009 the USA, which has only 5 times the population of the UK, scrapped a whopping 14 million cars, with much of the metal going to China.

Looking sideways at machine
It glancing back at me
Something more than motor
More than glass and metal

I'm sure I felt its mischief
So sure I saw it smile
In something of its driving
In town and country mile

www.unrealautos.com

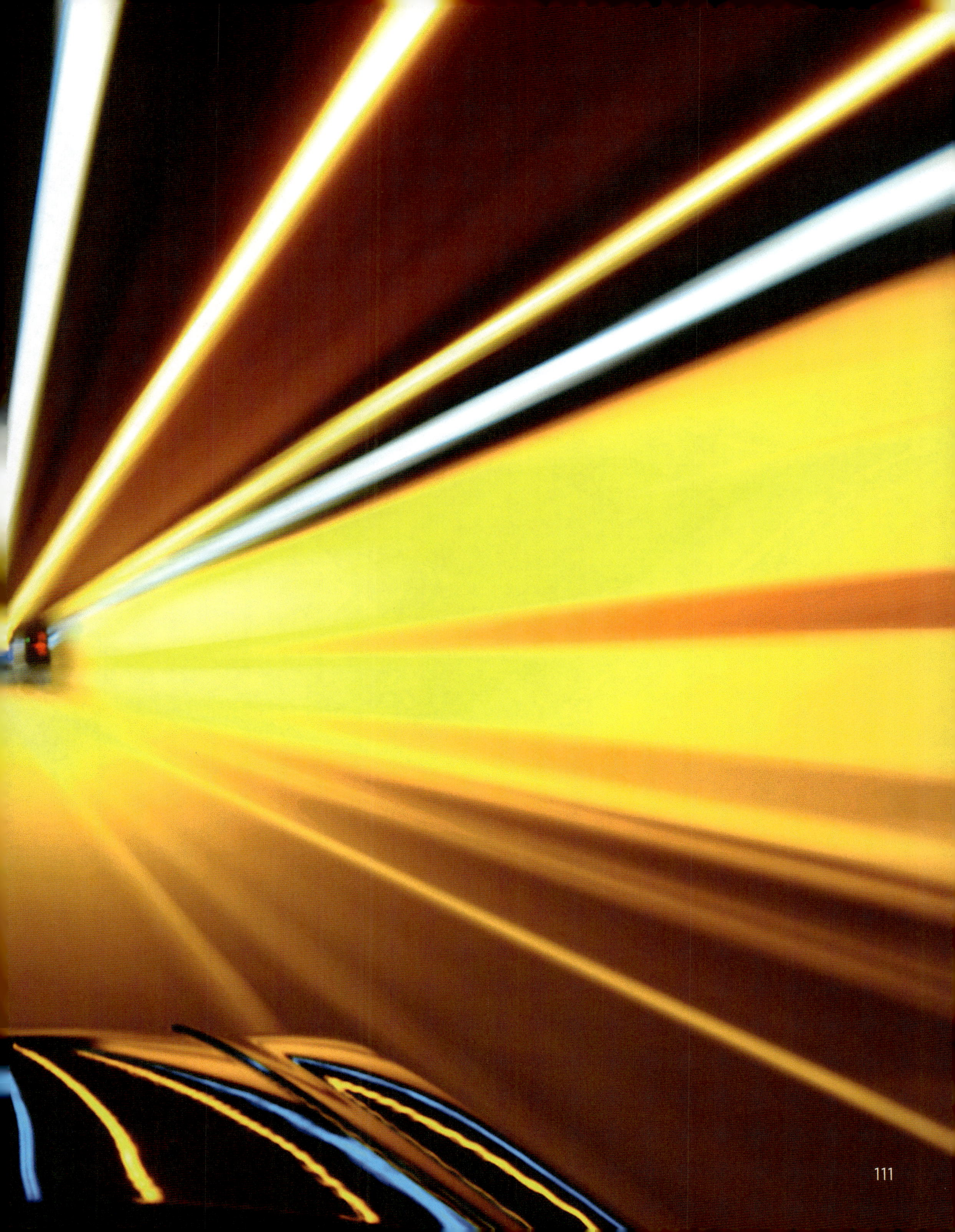

# CHAPTER 6
# TOP 5 FUTURISTIC CARS FROM SCI-FI FILMS

Many of you have been asking what are the most iconic, stylish, mean-looking and beautifully designed vehicles from the sci-fi genre of movies.

Ask no further, because here are our top 5 futuristic cars from film. These amazing vehicles are either real, albeit modified, production cars or bespoke concept designs. See if you recognize any of these from your favourite sci-fi movies.

www.unrealautos.com

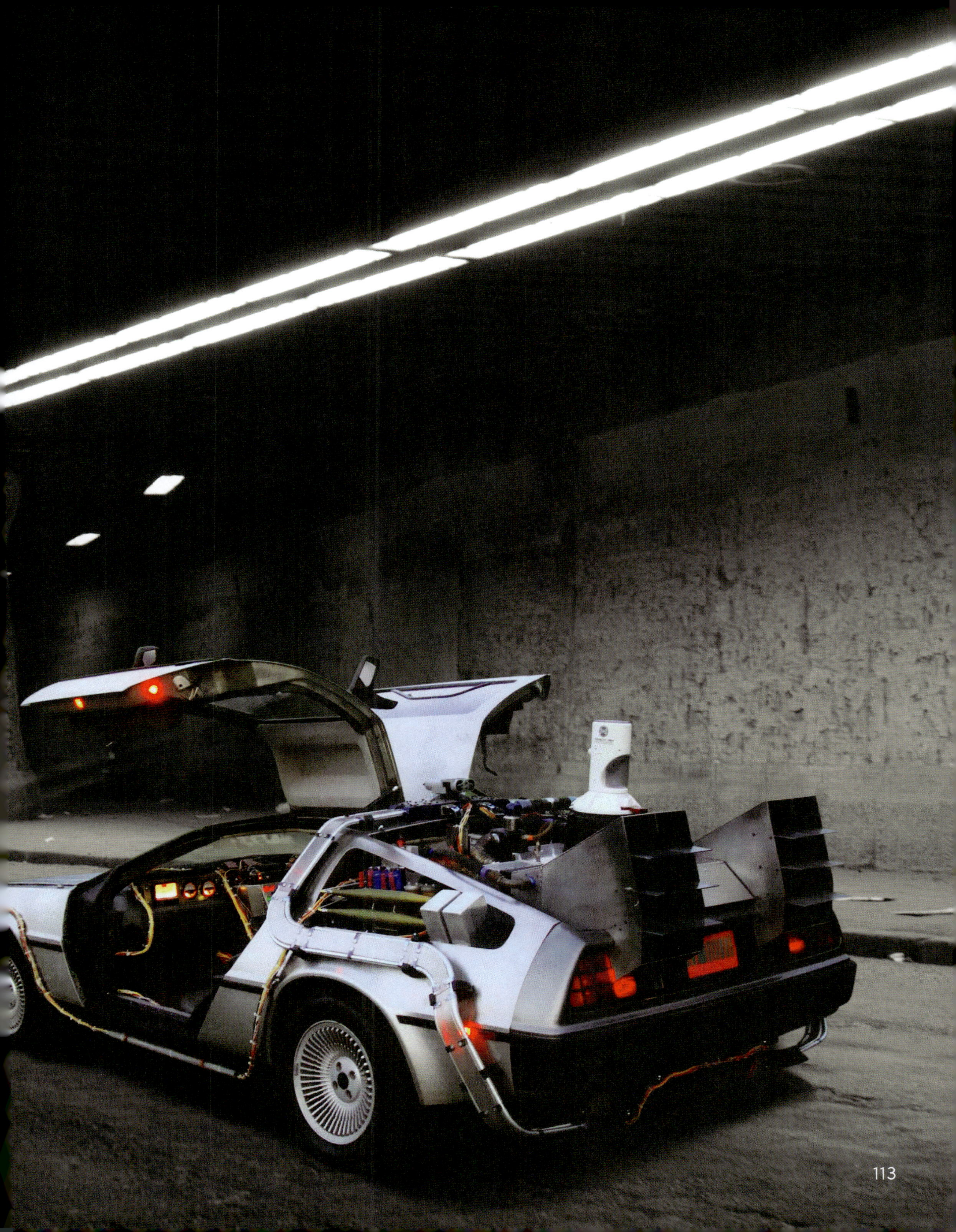

# 5.

## LEXUS CONCEPT MADE FOR SPIELBERG'S MINORITY REPORT (2002)

In at no. 5 comes a thing of such beauty, that it's worth bearing in mind it was more than just special effects.
    When Lexus fan Steven Spielberg approached the company for a specially commissioned concept, this is what Lexus gave him. What a piece of sculpture!

www.unrealautos.com

115

www.unrealautos.com

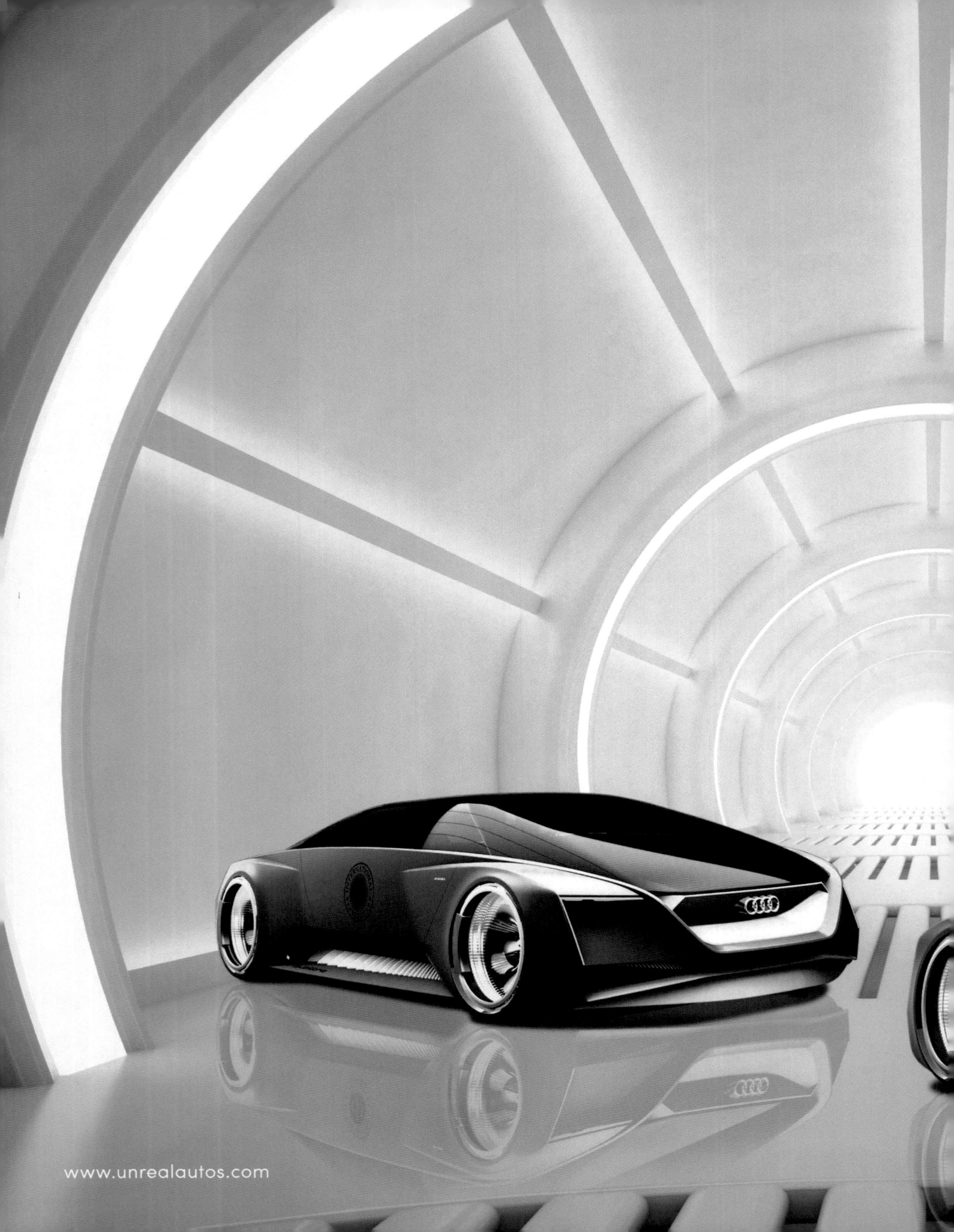

# 4.
## AUDI FLEET SHUTTLE QUATTRO (2013)

Sharp enough to bring tears to your eyes, Audi have used their virtual reality debut to bring a CGI car to the new, hot-off-the-presses film adaptation of Ender's Game. Is that a nuclear glow emitting from those pimp-my-grandson's-ride wheels? Who can say, but with quattro handling it's sure to go far. The green cab almost makes it look like the passengers are under water and it has more gills along the running boards than a shark. This is one concept that won't be sinking though.

www.unrealautos.com

# 3.
## FORD INTERCEPTOR (2014)

The story behind the new Ford for Mad Max: Fury Road, due out in 2015, is itself unusual. They actually developed two concepts to put them out to public vote, to see which one will finally appear in the film. On this page we have the Brookliner, and on the left, the NiMachine. See which Interceptor you like best. They're both absolutely rocking. It's a pity it doesn't look like Mel Gibson will be at the wheel.

# 2.
## THE BOMBPROOF BATMOBILE IN BATMAN (1989)

We had to give you at least one batmobile from one of the Batman films. Today, fans still talk about the 1960s car but there is one classic scene from the 1989 outing that is worthy of a reminder.

How awesome is a car that drops a bomb from its hubcap and is then so protected by its own shields that the building around it blows up, but the car is left unharmed.

www.unrealautos.com

DOWNLOAD THESE PHOTOS AS DESKTOP WALLPAPERS OR POSTERS

Go to www.unrealautos.com/wallpapers

# 1.
## DELOREAN FROM BACK TO THE FUTURE (1985)

In 1st place it could only be one car and one film. The atomic DeLorean at the heart of the mad doc's schemes was the first time many cinema-goers had seen time travelled in such gull-winged style.

Interestingly, four of the ten cars in our original list were the brainchild of one man – Jay Ohrberg, from whom we get KITT (Knight Rider), the Panthermobile, the Batmobile and the modified DeLorean. To see the cars that didn't make our list and vote for your favourite, visit www.unrealautos.com.

Now if we can just get it up to 88 mph...

www.unrealautos.com

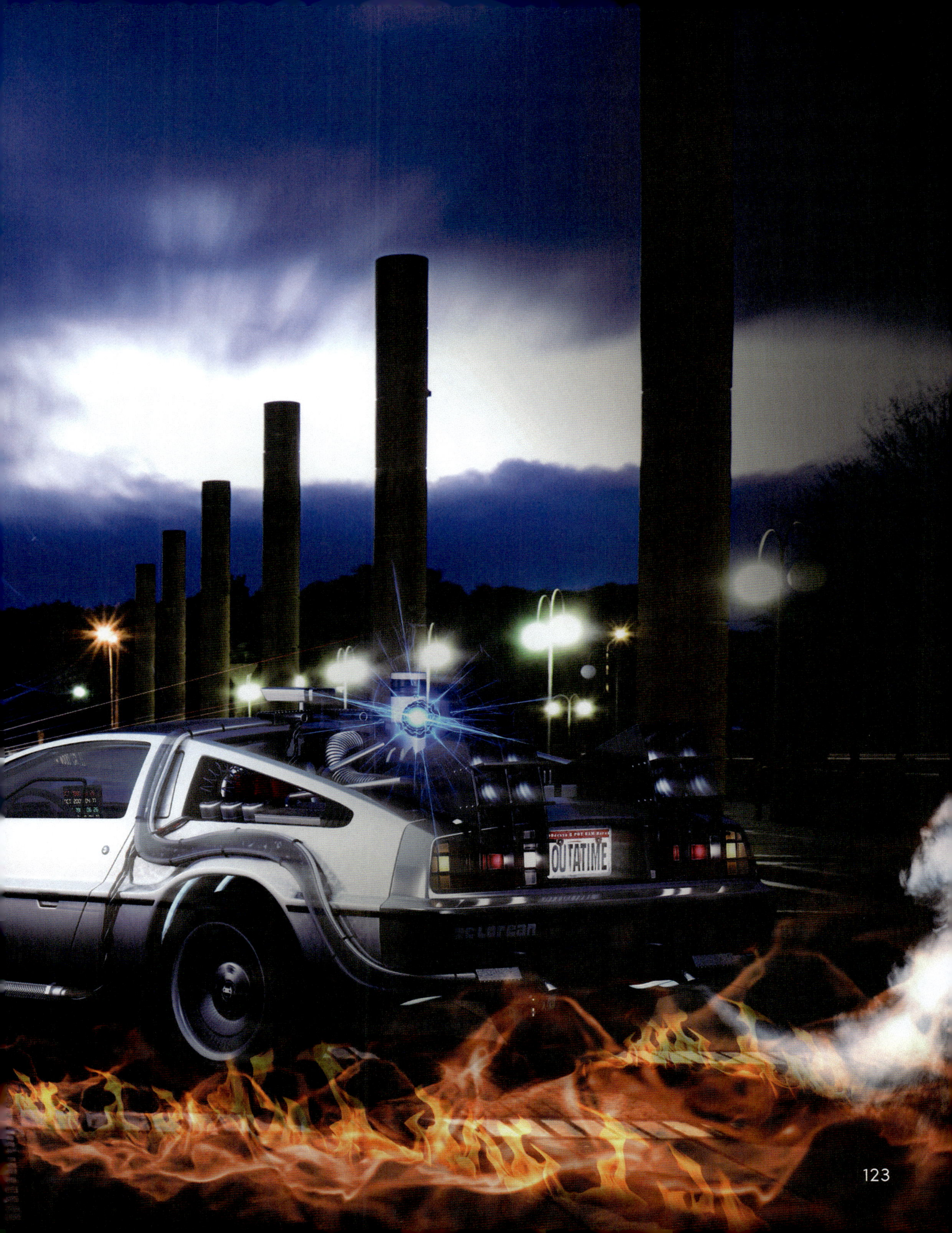
OUTATIME

## The Beast

President Obama's official armoured limousine, 'The Beast', has inch-thick windows to render it bulletproof. On a visit to Ireland, an identical support limo in the presidential cavalcade beached itself on the kerb while leaving the US Embassy in Dublin, blocking The Beast in behind it.

www.unrealautos.com

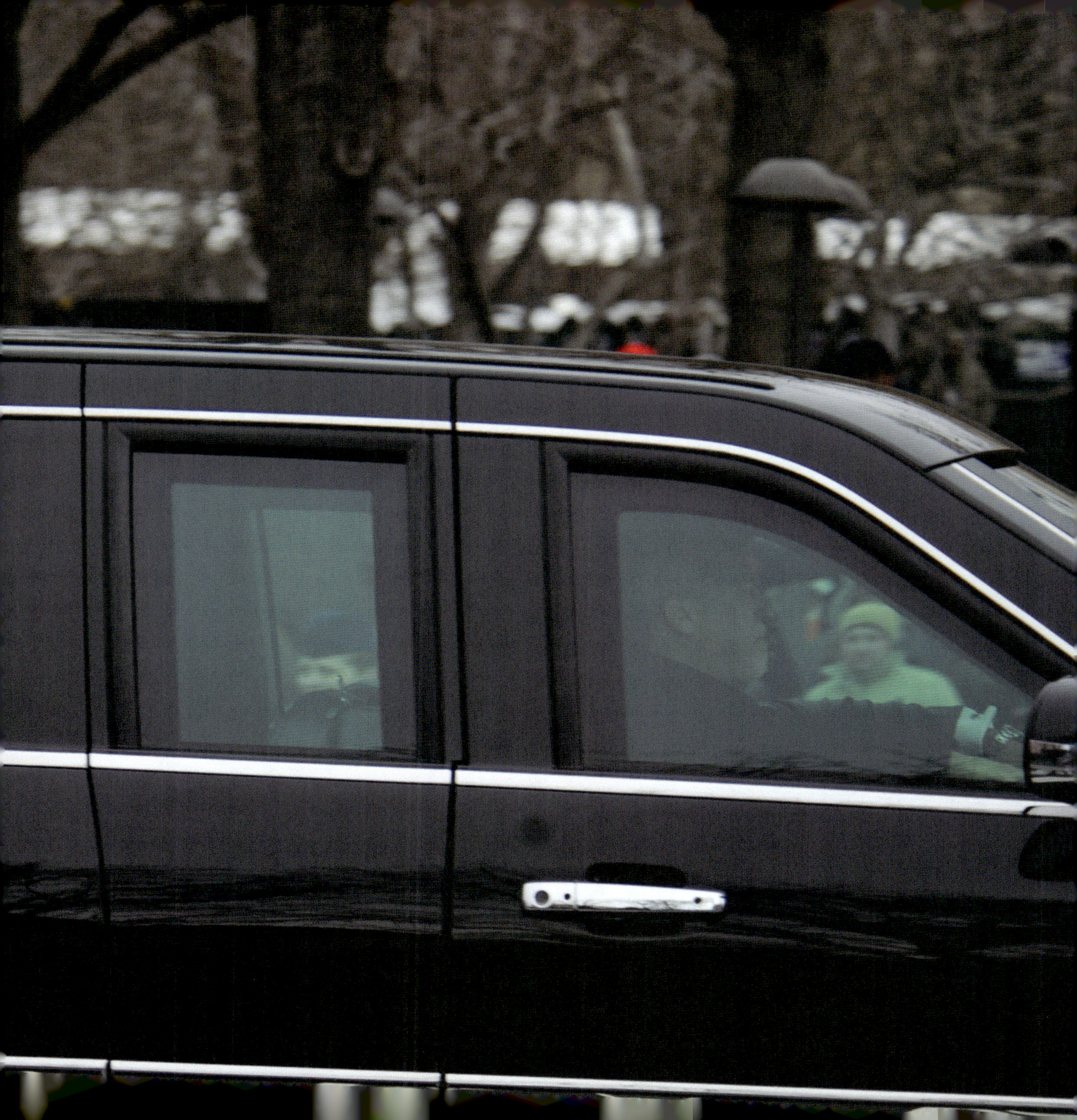

## Is it a car?
## Is it an airship?

If you had been around in Britain or Europe during either of the world wars, you would have seen cars, buses and trucks with large gas bags above their rooves. Petrol (gasoline) was so short that some people adapted their motor vehicles to run off coal gas instead.

www.unrealautos.com

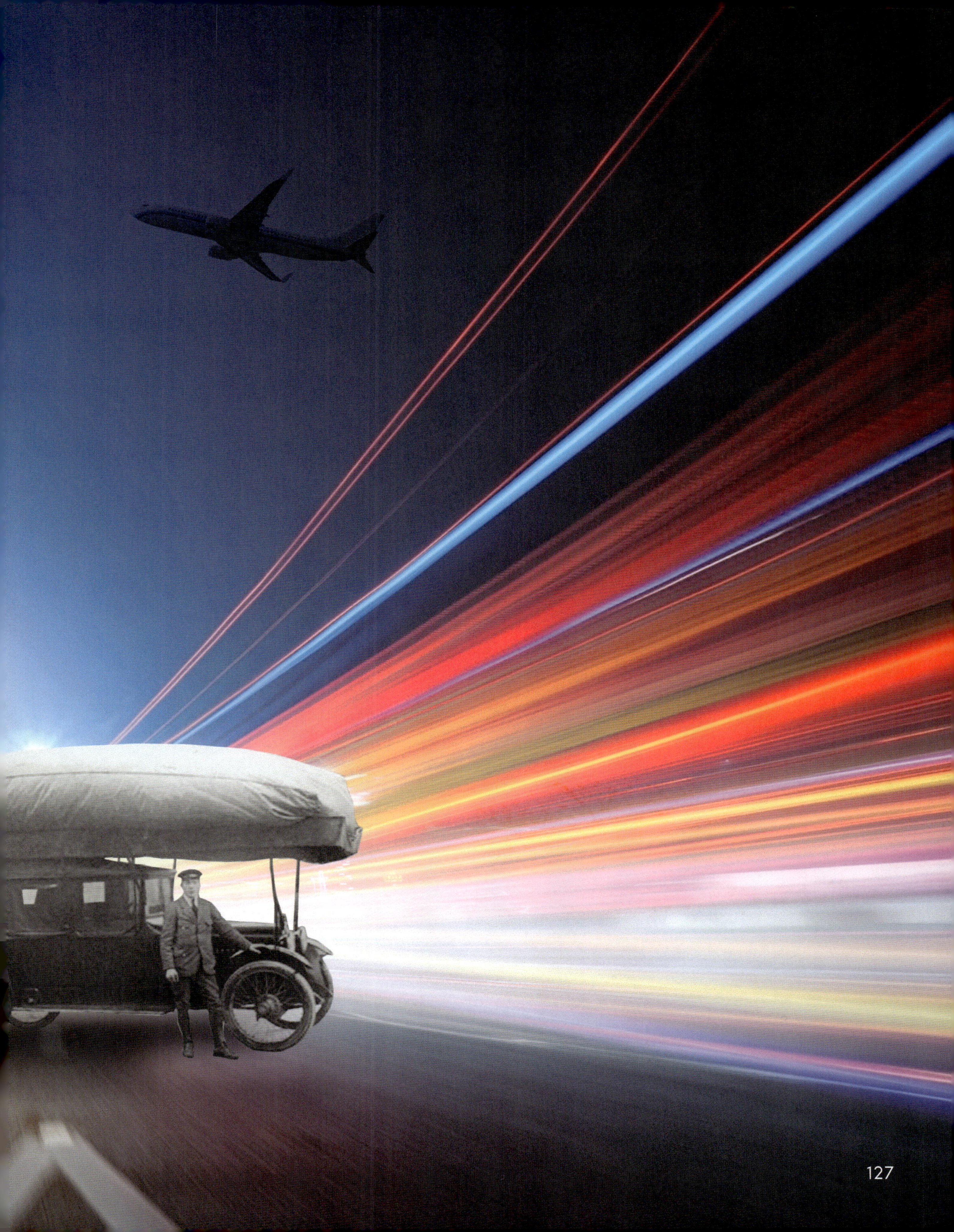

www.unrealautos.com

## CHAPTER 7
# WHEN WILL WE HAVE A FLYING CAR?

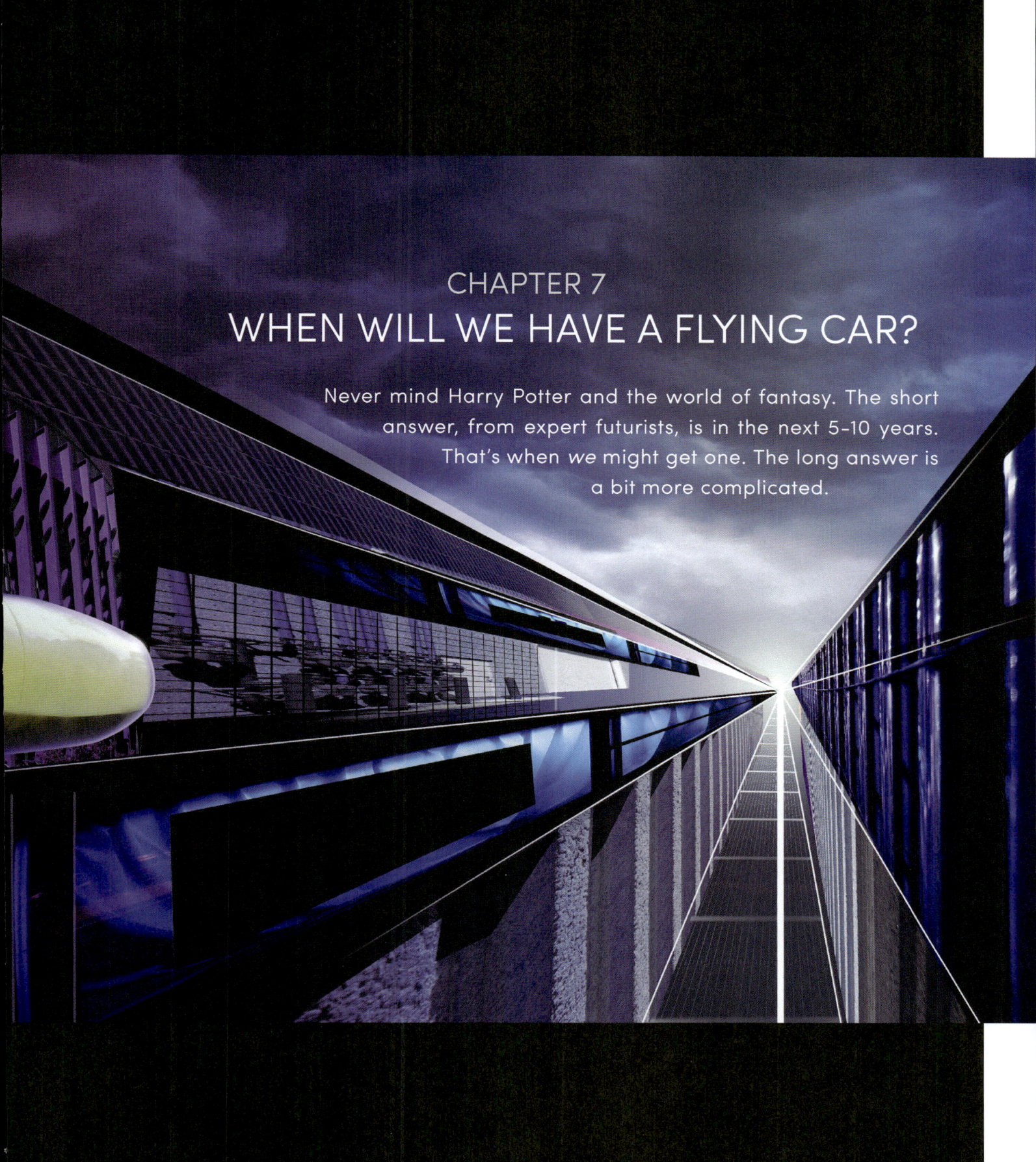

Never mind Harry Potter and the world of fantasy. The short answer, from expert futurists, is in the next 5-10 years. That's when *we* might get one. The long answer is a bit more complicated.

## WHAT DO WE MEAN?

Well, the technology is one thing, and you're going to see, from some of the prototypes already working, that the flying car is technically here already. It's really a question of obstacles and solutions.

www.unrealautos.com

# OBSTACLES & SOLUTIONS

There are a few things in the way of you – or your neighbour – actually being able to buy one and use it at home. When will flying cars become approved, mass-produced, manageable and affordable?

How will we get around those problems?

If it has wings and rotors for cruising the skies, it needs to retract those wings and have engine-driven wheels when it's on the ground, sharing narrow space with oncoming road-users.

AEROMOBIL 2.5 FOLDS ITS WINGS
BACK FOR ROAD TRAVEL

AEROMOBIL.COM

## ENERGY CONSUMPTION & COSTS

Although most flying cars we're showing you have retractable wings, here's one that uses a motor and parachute much like an ultralight. The SkyRunner has the advantage of being able to glide slowly in to land in the event of an emergency.

It also means less energy is consumed as it's just a light weight buggy, aided by wind power and a little extra lift from the engine. Other fixed-wing flying cars are likely to spend quite a bit of your cash in fuel.

It's also worth saying that many more elaborate flying cars come with aeroplane price tags over £100,000.

ANDRECARS.COM

*THE DORSET-BUILT PARAJET SKYRUNNER CAN DO 55 MPH IN THE AIR*

## MAINTENANCE & SERVICING

Okay, so all of the designers of serious flying cars still have to approach this problem of making a machine suitable for flying and driving in the same unit. But that doesn't just apply to design; it affects the maintenance and servicing needs too.

Think of all the extra parts you'll need looking over. It doesn't matter too much if your car breaks down on the road and you have to pull over; but how do you find the hard shoulder up on Cloud 9? Flight takes travel safety to a whole new level.

TERRAFUGIA.COM / DRIVENTOFLY.COM

www.unrealautos.com

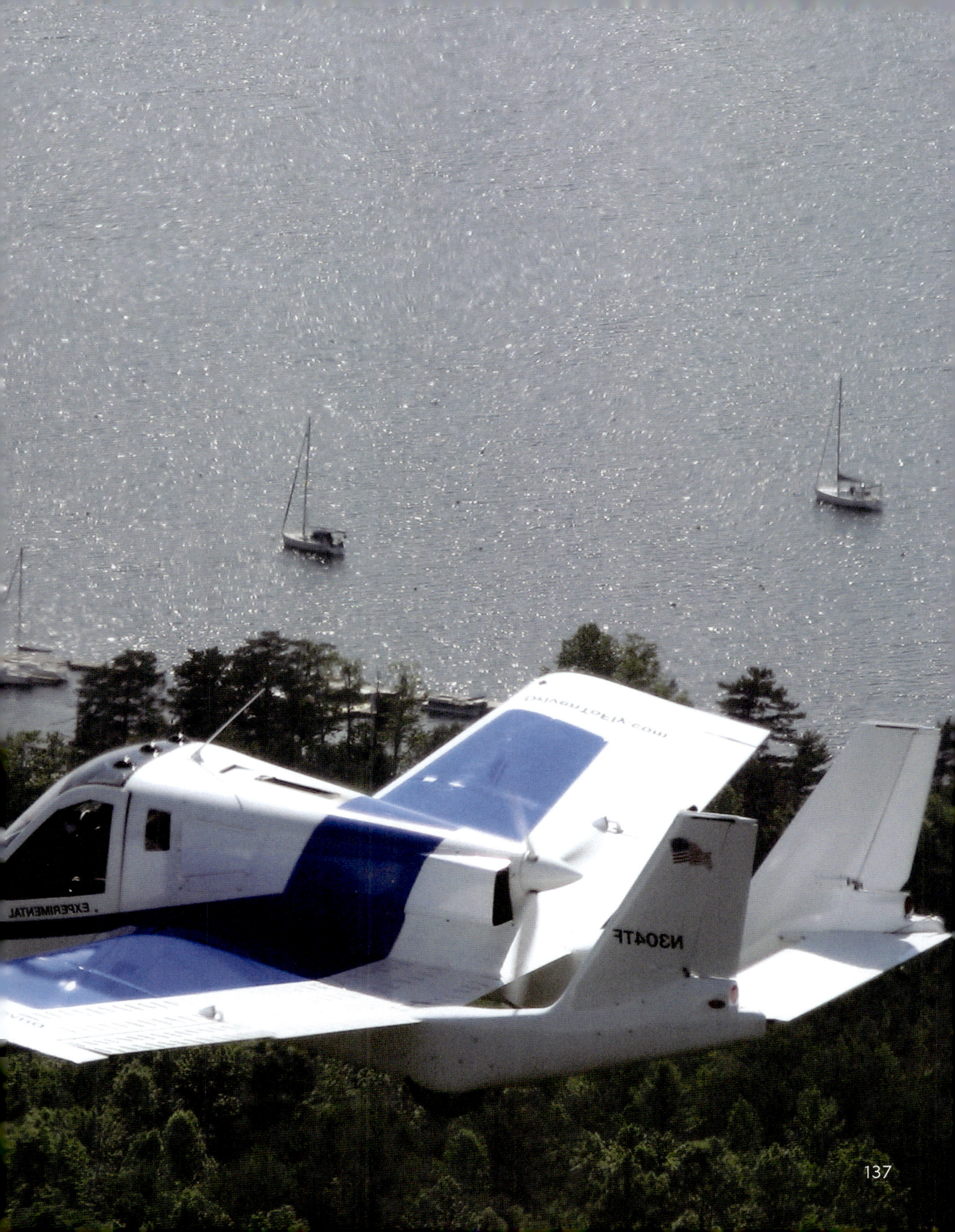

## TRAINING & LICENSING

Learning to drive a car is one thing. Learning to fly a plane is much more involved, harder and expensive; but what about learning to control something that does both?

All of these issues will have to be worked out with national governments, their civil aviation authorities like the UK CAA and US FAA, and finally, national road transport authorities.

www.unrealautos.com

139

At least the serious flying car-makers are planning automated computer flying to help the novice get going. We leave you with the TF-X Concept from Terrafugia with extending wings, automatic flight and vertical take-off.

So yes, the flying car is really here now, but look out for newer, more automated-flying models in a few years time that will make it safer and more affordable. Until then, safe dreaming!

TERRAFUGIA.COM / DRIVENTOFLY.COM

www.unrealautos.com

*THE TERRAFUGIA TF-X CONCEPT NEEDS NO RUNWAY AND DOES IT ALL FOR YOU*

# Breathing cars

Car engines need 14.7 litres of air for every 1 litre of fuel vapour they combust. That's why they struggle to keep going at the highest altitudes.

www.unrealautos.com

143

# CHAPTER 8
## TOP 10 TIPS FROM PROFESSIONAL RACERS

Brace yourself for our run-down of top driving tips from the greats of motorsport. We've gathered together the condensed wisdom from Formula 1 Season Champions, IndyCar heroes, Le Mans winners and more besides.

Are you ready? Go!

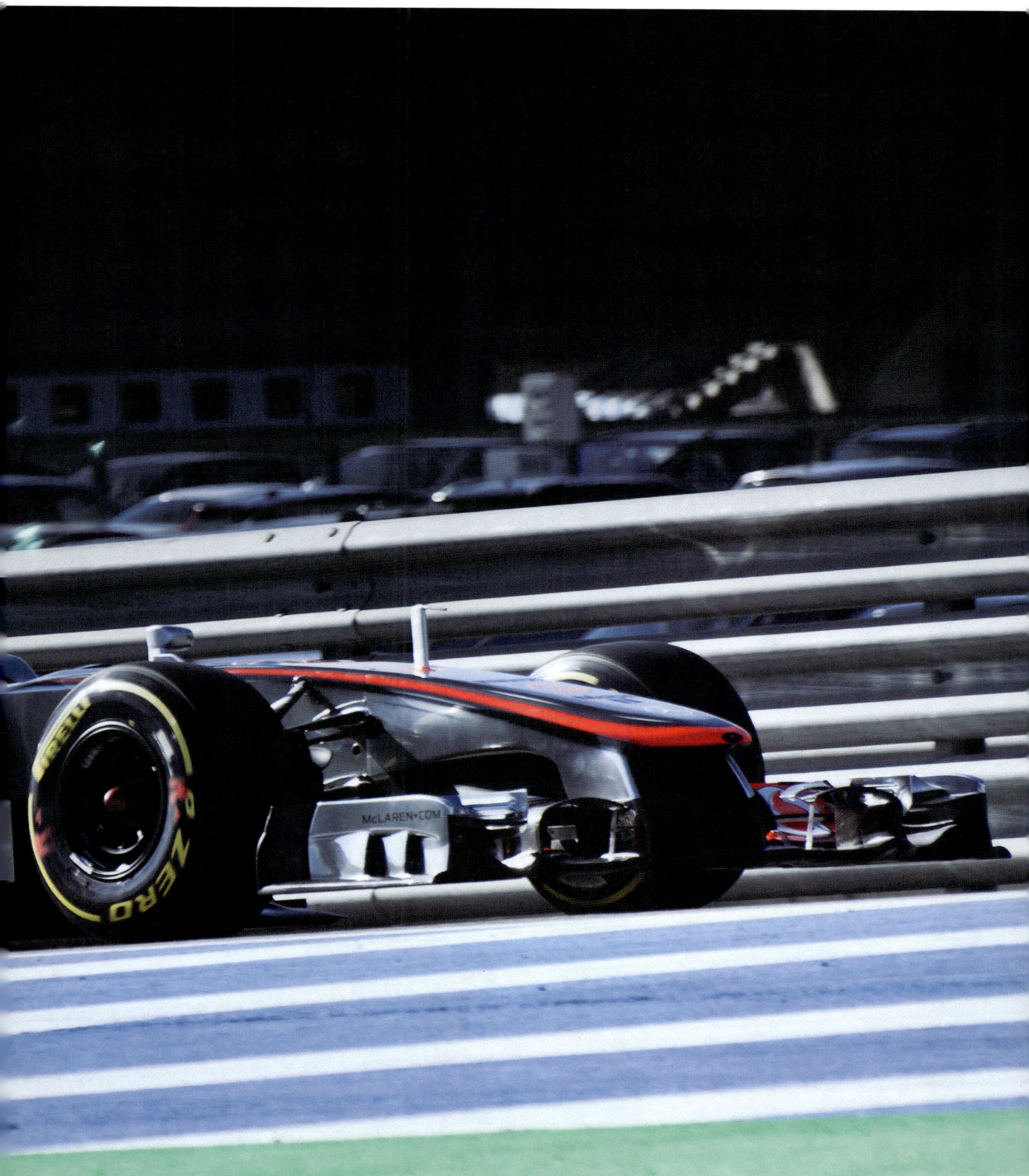
McLAREN•COM
ZERO

# 10.
## USE A HIGHER GEAR IN WINTRY CONDITIONS - JAMES NASH

World Touring Car star, James Nash, has a winter driving tip for you. Use a higher gear, which uses more torque, and thus reduces your risk of wheel-spinning and loss of grip on slippy road surfaces. It could reduce your fuel consumption as well as lessening your chances of losing control during acceleration.

www.unrealautos.com

14
J. Nash
Champion
ultracommerce
LASER
ecm
YOKOHAMA
GoPro
Be a HERO.
HILLS
www.bamboo-engineering com

# 9.

## IMPROVE YOUR AWARENESS – JENSON BUTTON

British F1 winner Jenson Button wants you to improve your awareness of other road users ahead, behind, and to the side of you. Take heed to changing road conditions, and shifts in visibility, brought on by banks of fog or turning off onto minor roads.

www.unrealautos.com

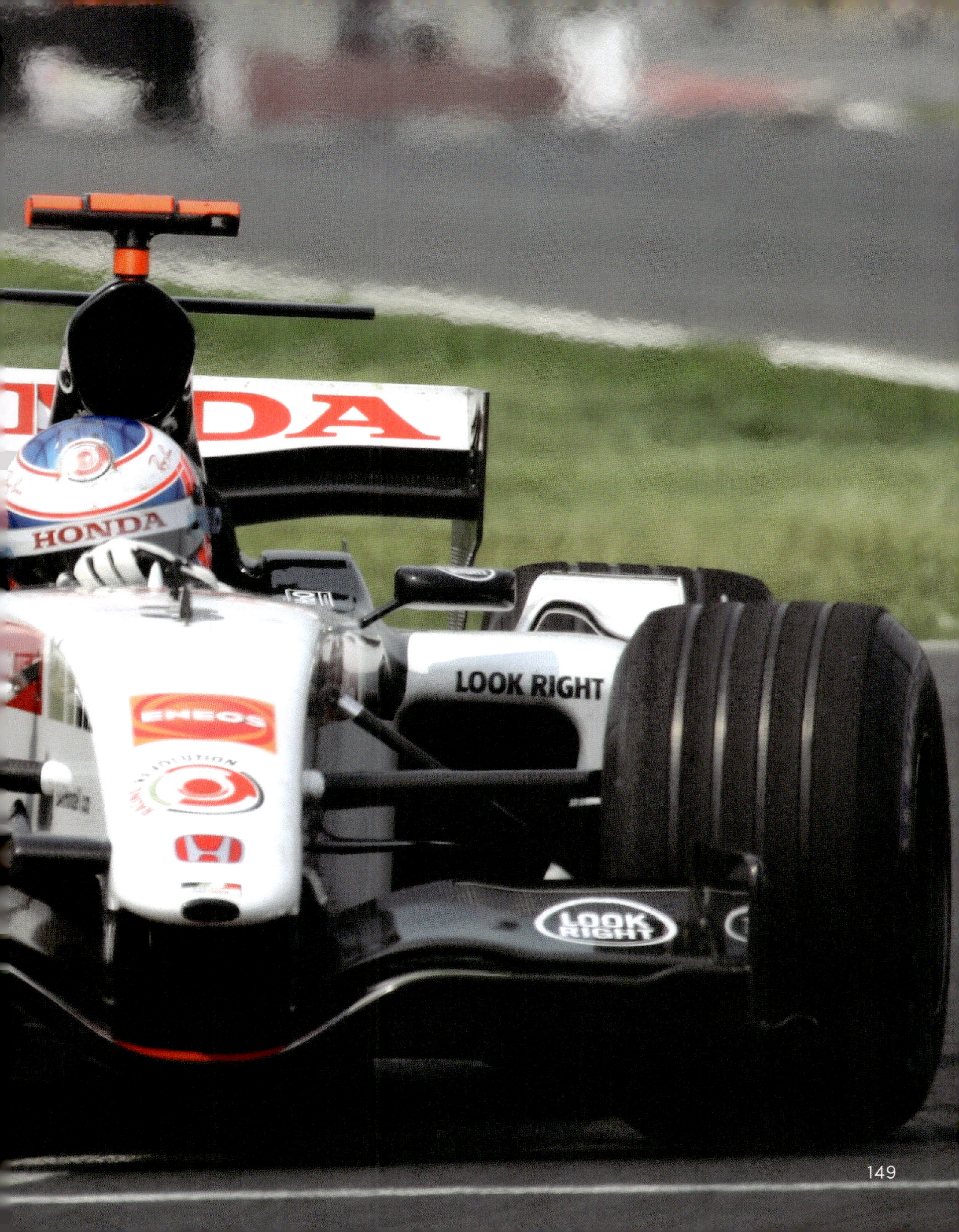
HONDA
LOOK RIGHT
ENEOS
LOOK RIGHT

www.unrealautos.com

# 8.
## SLOW DOWN – MIKA HÄKKINEN

Finnish racer Mika Häkkinen, F1 champ in 1998 and '99, says his top tip is to slow down. The Finns are masters at car control and Mika stresses that safe driving is very much about speed.

# 7.
## AVOID UNNECESSARY BRAKING – DAMON HILL

British F1 hero Damon Hill's eco-driving tip helps save the fuel wasted by unnecessary braking. Conserve momentum when approaching traffic lights, and predict their changes, along with those of fellow road users in your path.

www.unrealautos.com

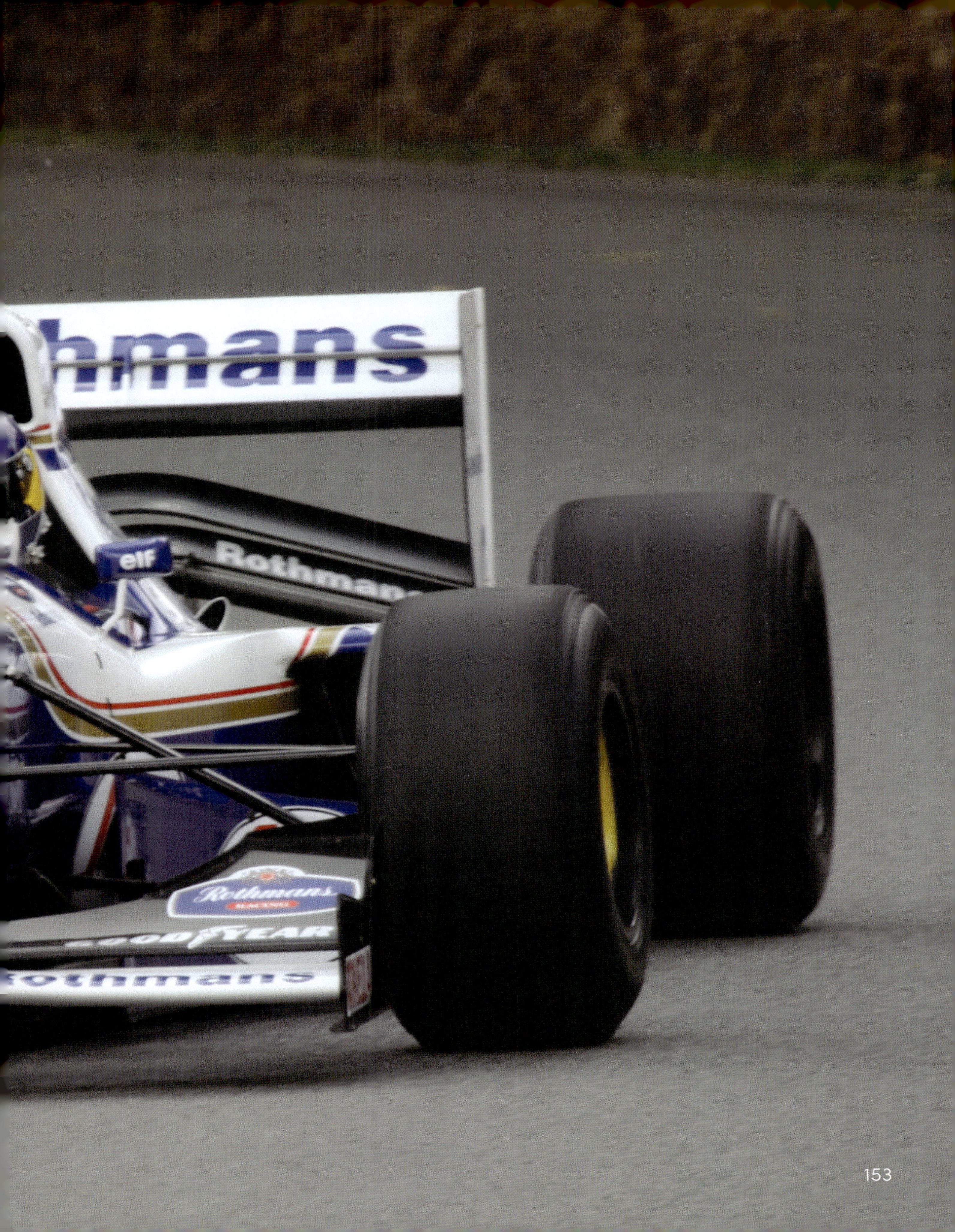
elf
Rothmans
RACING

# 6.
## MAKE TRANSITIONS SMOOTH – JACKIE STEWART

Jackie Stewart is the only British racer to win three F1 seasons. He recommends driving so as to make transitions imperceptible, between straight and turning, and braking and acceleration. It's better for grip – and passenger comfort.

www.unrealautos.com

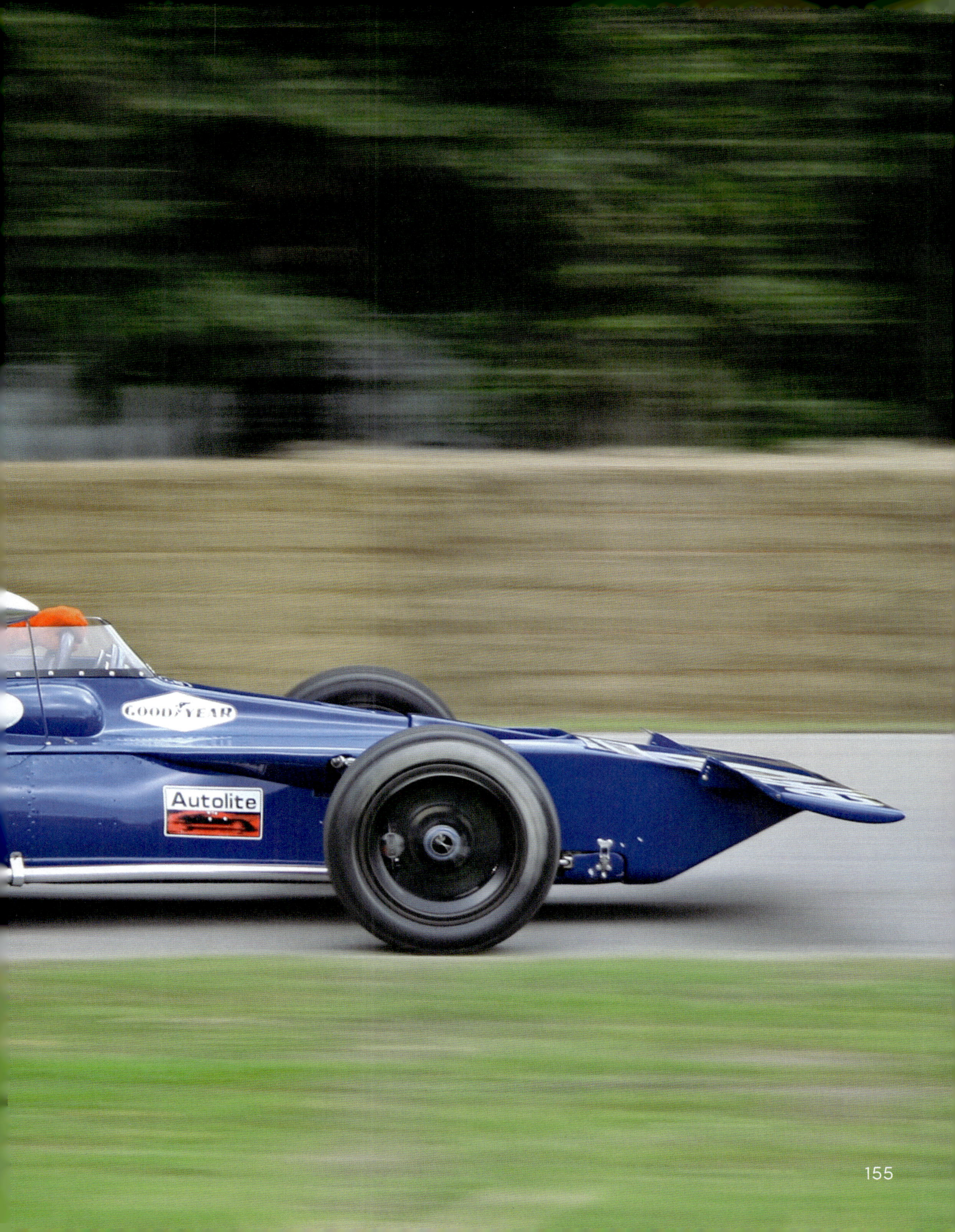
GOODYEAR
Autolite

www.unrealautos.com

# 5.
## STOP TAILGATING – JOHNNY O'CONNELL

Johnny O'Connell, IndyCar driver and four-time winner at Le Mans, thinks that some people have been watching too much NASCAR. They leave their TVs behind but take the driving style out onto the street. Stay well behind that car in front!

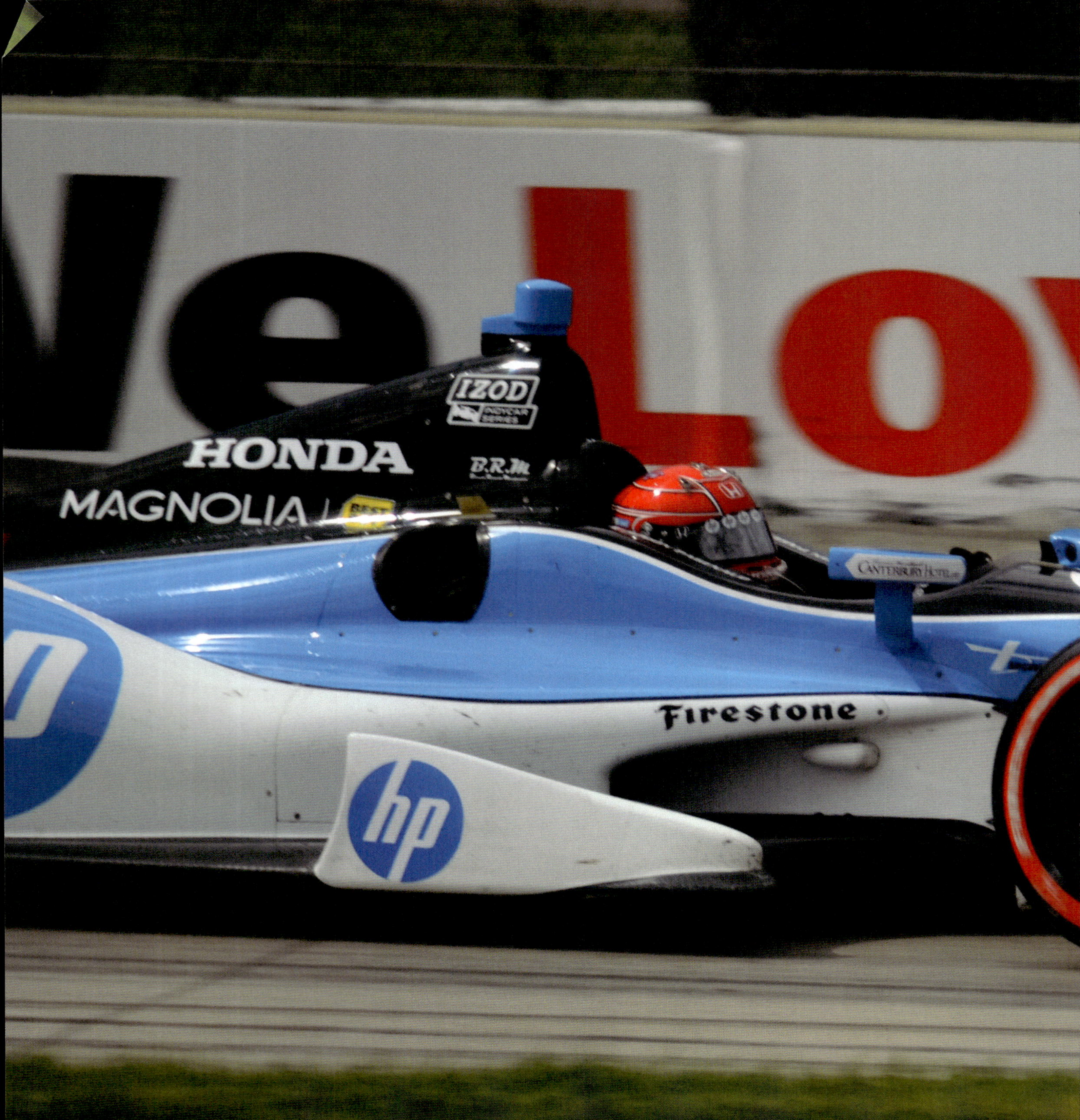
We
IZOD
HONDA
MAGNOLIA
Firestone
hp

# 4.

## HANDLE TYRE-BURSTS MORE SAFELY
## – SIMON PAGENAUD

Avoid a nasty uncontrolled collision, says LMP1 and Atlantic Championship winner, Simon Pagenaud. When a tyre bursts at speed don't just hit the brake hard. It's much safer to declutch and engage Neutral, then brake lightly.

# 3.
## TWO HANDS ON THE WHEEL ONCE IN GEAR – MARK WEBBER

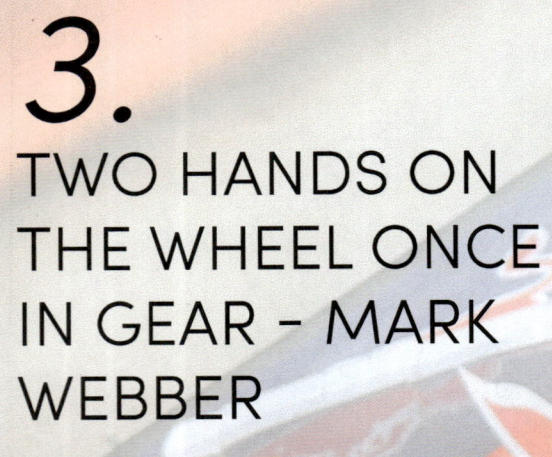

It sounds like beginners' stuff but when Mark Webber took fellow Red Bull team member Jon DeVore out on the track, he reminded him to keep two hands on the wheel. As soon as you've made that gear change, both hands back on. If anything happens like a wheel brush with a kerb at speed, you don't want the steering to fly out of your grip!

www.unrealautos.com

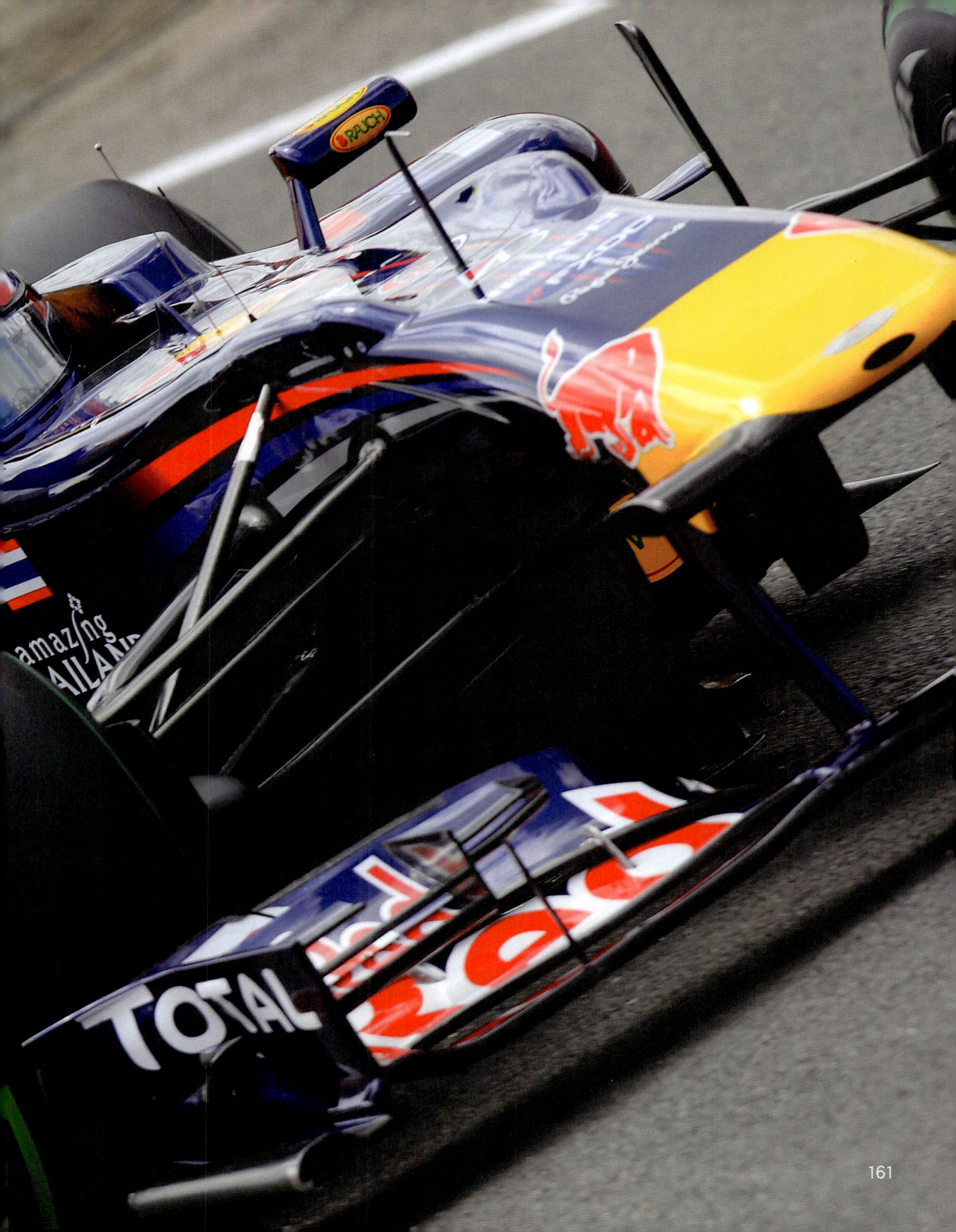
RAUCH
TOTAL

www.unrealautos.com

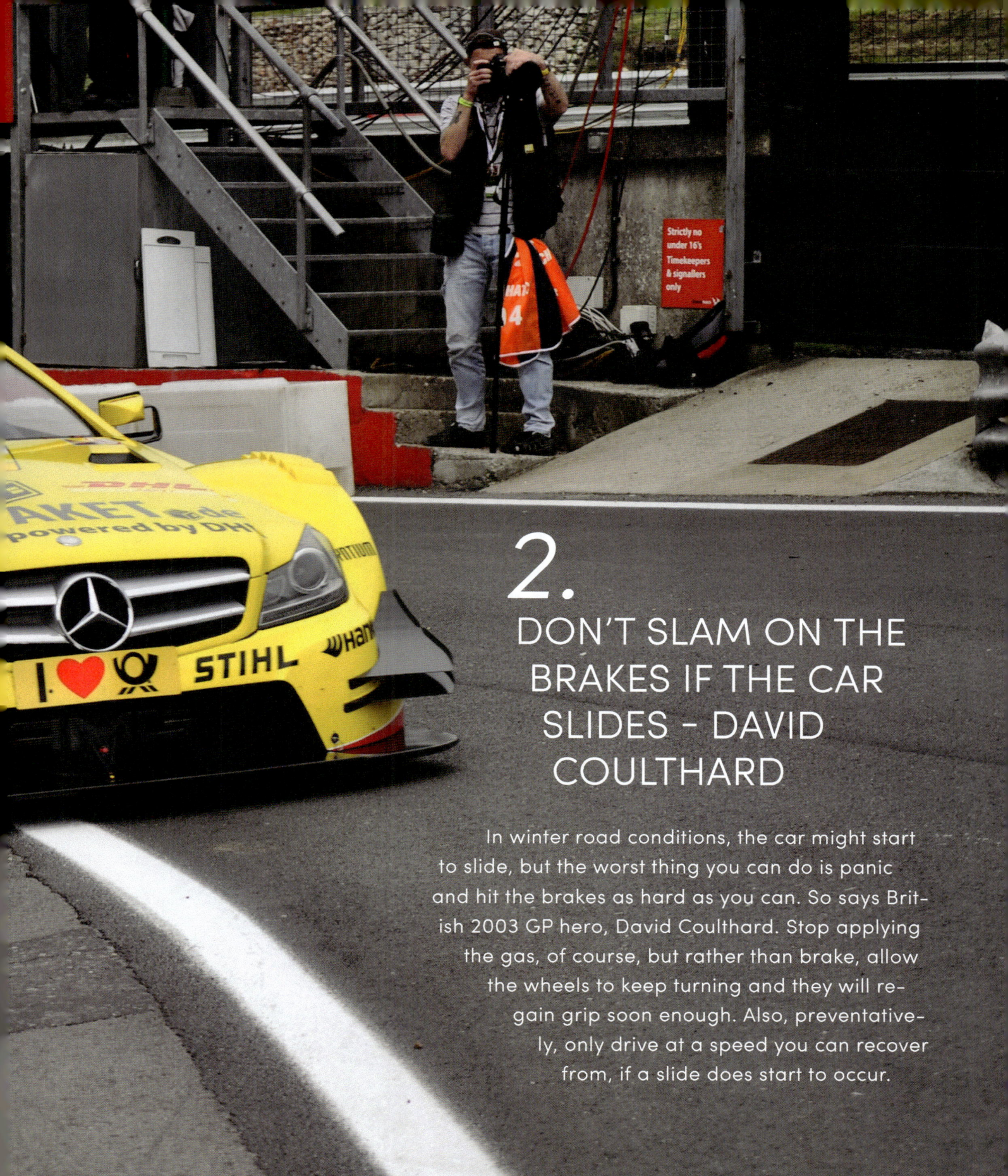

# 2.
## DON'T SLAM ON THE BRAKES IF THE CAR SLIDES - DAVID COULTHARD

In winter road conditions, the car might start to slide, but the worst thing you can do is panic and hit the brakes as hard as you can. So says British 2003 GP hero, David Coulthard. Stop applying the gas, of course, but rather than brake, allow the wheels to keep turning and they will regain grip soon enough. Also, preventatively, only drive at a speed you can recover from, if a slide does start to occur.

# 1.
## KNOW YOUR DRIVING LIMITS – MICHAEL SCHUMACHER

Statistically the most successful Formula 1 champion of all time Michael Schumacher says it's essential to know your driving limits, as well as those of the road and your vehicle. Knowledge is power – the power to stay in one piece.

www.unrealautos.com

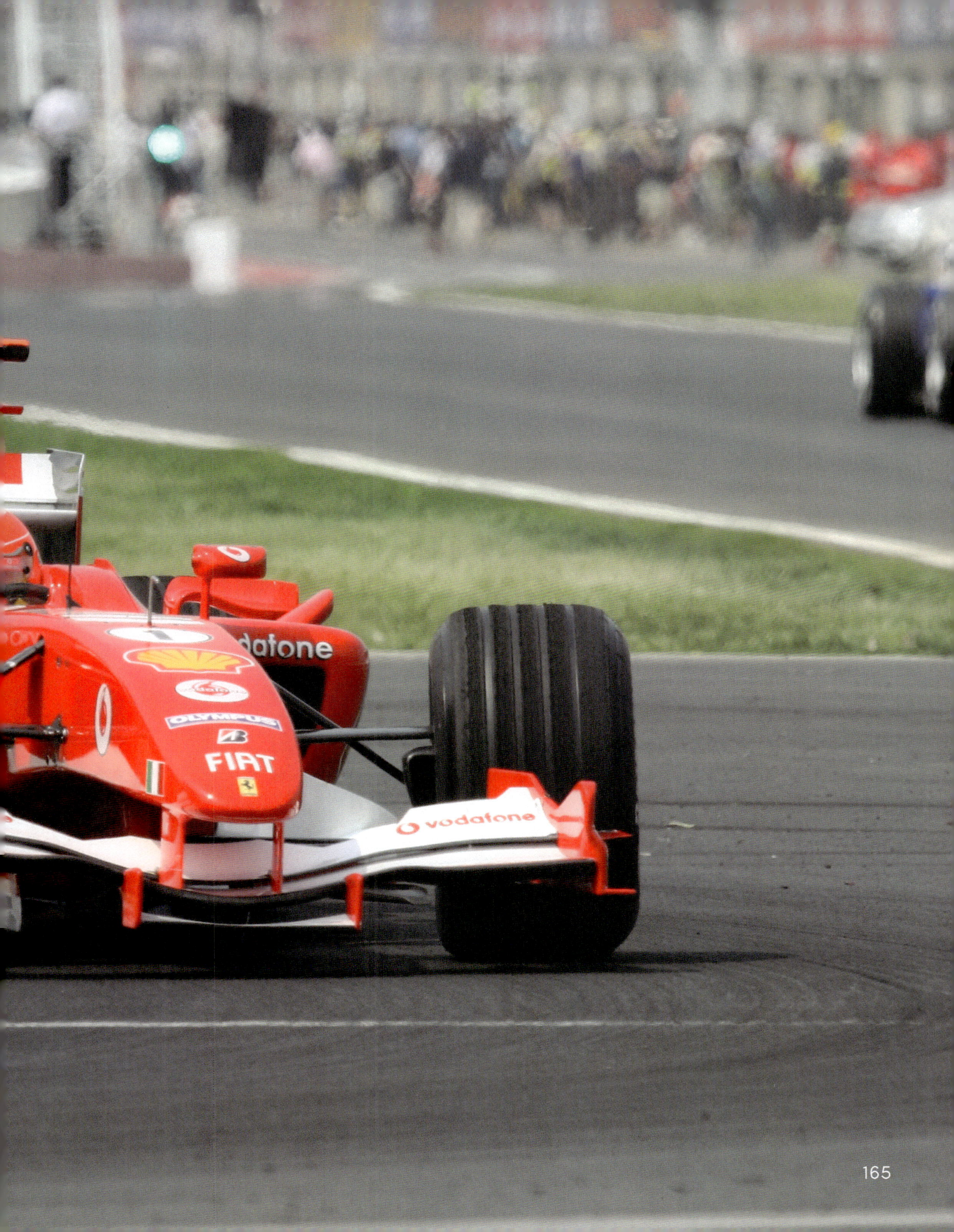
dafone
OLYMPUS
FIAT
vodafone

Noise is all around me
Engines screaming
Crowds are shouting

Flash bulbs a plenty
For tomorrow's back pages

Men by my sides
Chomping at the bit
Wishing they were
Where I was

But for me all is silent
Save my own car and racing pulse
All is black
Save the starting lights ahead
And the track is empty
Save the beast underfoot

Every second lasts a minute
Every minute lasts an hour
The lights change
The sword of Damocles drops

www.unrealautos.com

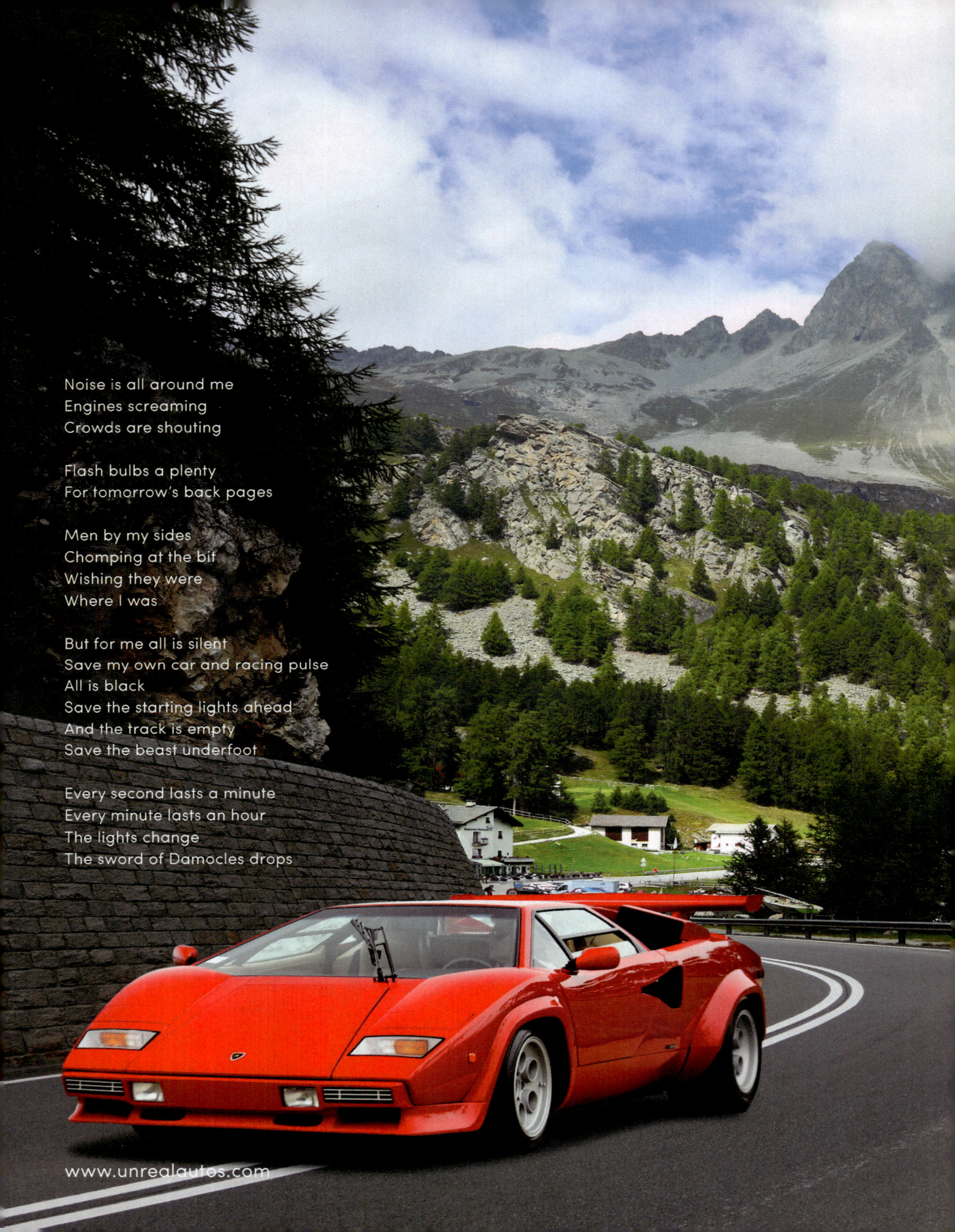

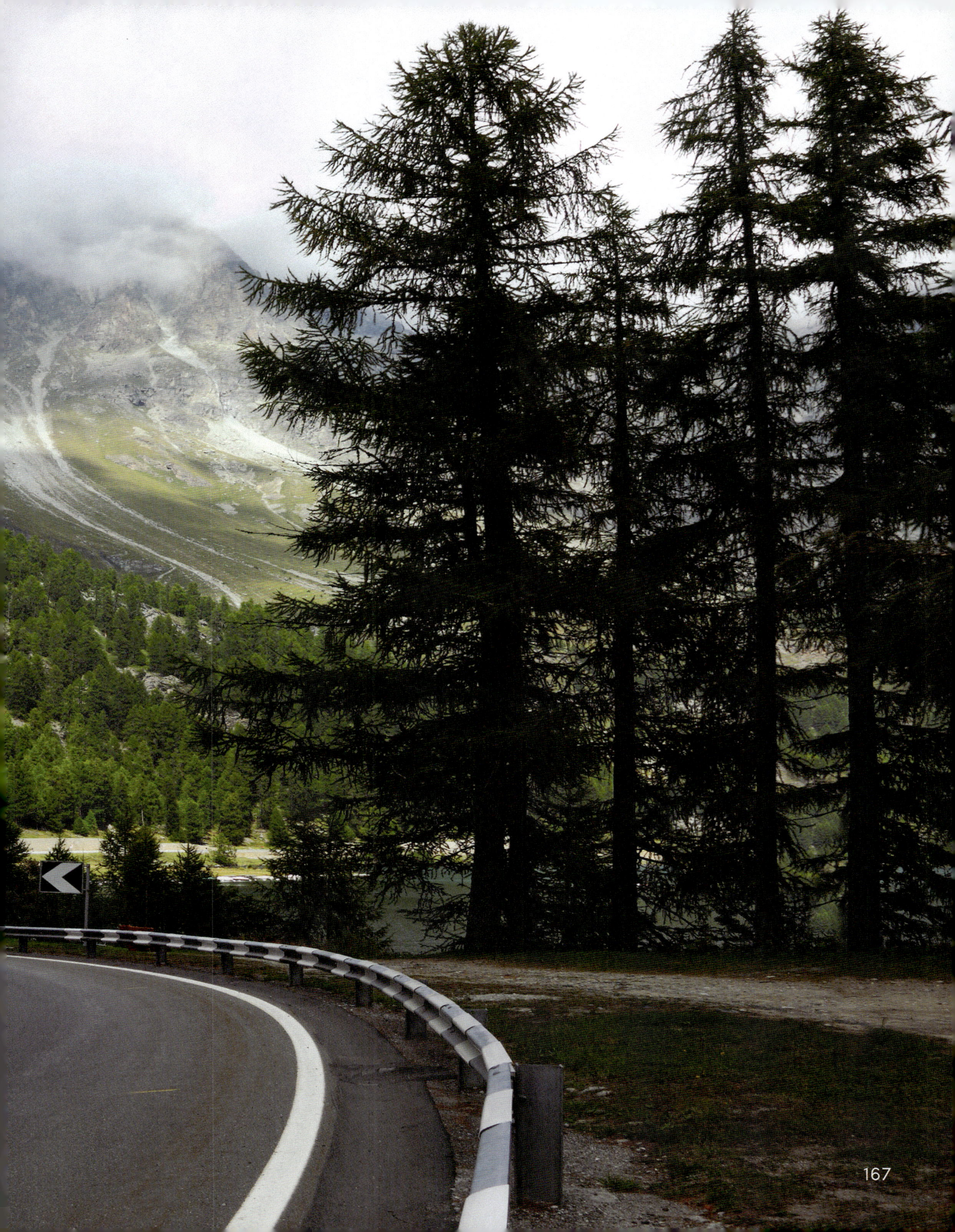

www.unrealautos.com

# CHAPTER 9
## TOP 5 IN-CAR GADGETS

You're never going to believe some of the cool gadgets that are out there to enhance your in-car experience. It wasn't so long ago that the most useful thing to pop into your car's 12V power socket was a cigar lighter.

Today though the sky's the limit – and it's all much easier on the lungs. The tech is bordering on the futuristic in some cases and it's doing everything from giving you journey information whilst keeping your eyes on the road, to that strong cuppa to help keep you alert. Take a sneaky peek at what we mean...

www.unrealautos.com

## 5.
## HEAD-UP DISPLAY

The future is here and important journey information like the car's speed can now be beamed onto the windscreen much like the helmet HUD in a fighter jet. The safety benefits of not having to avert your gaze from the road are pretty obvious, but think of how much you can impress your passengers too.

www.unrealautos.com

# 4.
## BANG & OLUFSEN ACOUSTIC LENSES

Jezza on Top Gear once got very excited about these, but then he loves anything by B&O. These futuristic audio speakers rise from the fascia when in use and disappear again when not. The retractable delectables enable a listener to hear optimum sound regardless of their location within the vehicle.

# 3.
# GOOGLE GLASS

While not specifically a car gadget, Google Glass promises to deliver a head-up information and communication experience that's just like the HUD above, but will move as your head moves. The jury's still out on the pros and cons of driver safety while using Google Glass, but just imagine being a passenger and pushing back in your seat while seeing the scenery fly by to the accompaniment of StreetView-style labels, restaurant reviews and audio track information. Scary or what?!

www.unrealautos.com

WITH GOOGLE GLASS YOU GET A HEAD-UP DISPLAY RIGHT
IN FRONT OF YOUR RIGHT EYE, JUST AS YOU SEE HERE

175

www.unrealautos.com

## 2.
### HANDPRESSO AUTO COFFEE-MAKER

Another lighter socket-powered gizmo, this attractive unit makes a proper high-pressure espresso from the convenience of a road lay-by. Caffeine, that great fuel of the long-distance driver, is now available without leaving your vehicle or paying a motorway service station for the privilege of fleecing you.

**WWW.** DISCOVER MORE WORLD-CLASS PREMIUM CAR ACCESSORIES ONLINE AT UNREALAUTOS.COM

Go to www.unrealautos.com/shop

# 1.
## NISSAN NISMO WATCH

Check out Nissan's latest piece of arm candy. That reassuring brand of Japanese reliability has come up with an ingenious way of prompting you to keep on top of your car's – and your body's – vital statistics. Aside from looking very different to your average wristwatch, the Nismo (see what they did there – Nissan/gizmo?) reminds you about loads of useful stuff from fuel level and wiper fluid to tyre status and where you parked the car. It even monitors your brainwaves, heart activity and skin temperature!

www.unrealautos.com

## That's long!
The longest street-legal, limited-production car ever made was the 1931 Bugatti Royale Type 41. At 6.4m (21ft) long, spare a thought for its drivers in the days before parking sensors were invented!

CHAPTER 10
# TOP 10 MOST BEAUTIFUL CARS BY DECADE

You can judge cars by power, control, price, size and safety. This list, though, is all about the looks. Some cars were considered classics in their time. Others achieved cult status many years later. What is history's verdict on the beautiful from each period of automotive history?

www.unrealautos.com

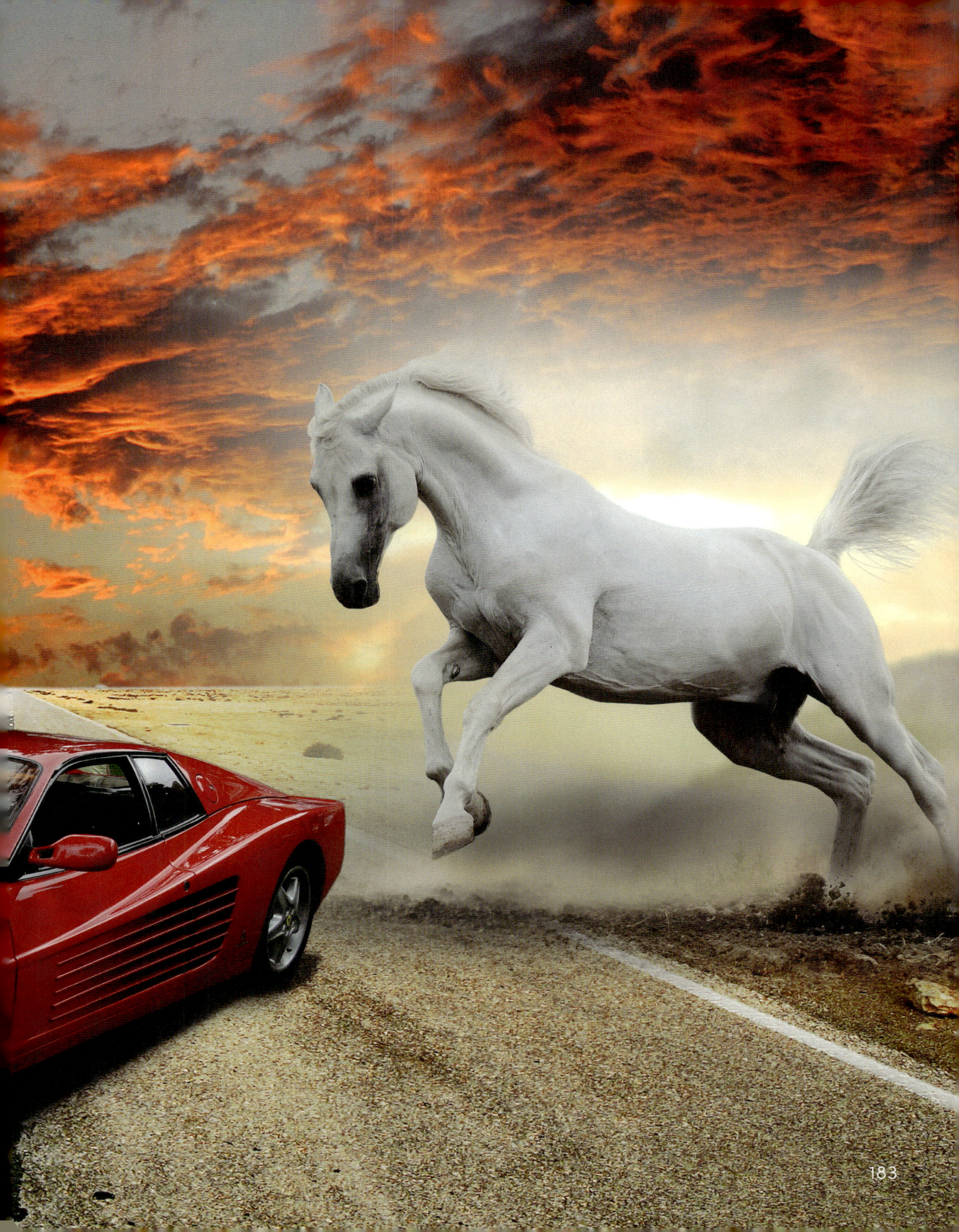

## BEAUTY IS IN THE EYE OF THE BEHOLDER

If you ask a car enthusiast from America you'll get a very different answer about what makes a pretty motor than if you asked a European, so we've tried to reflect as wide a range of tastes and nationalities as possible. These cars are, as we see it, the most beautiful car of each decade, starting with the '20's...

www.unrealautos.com

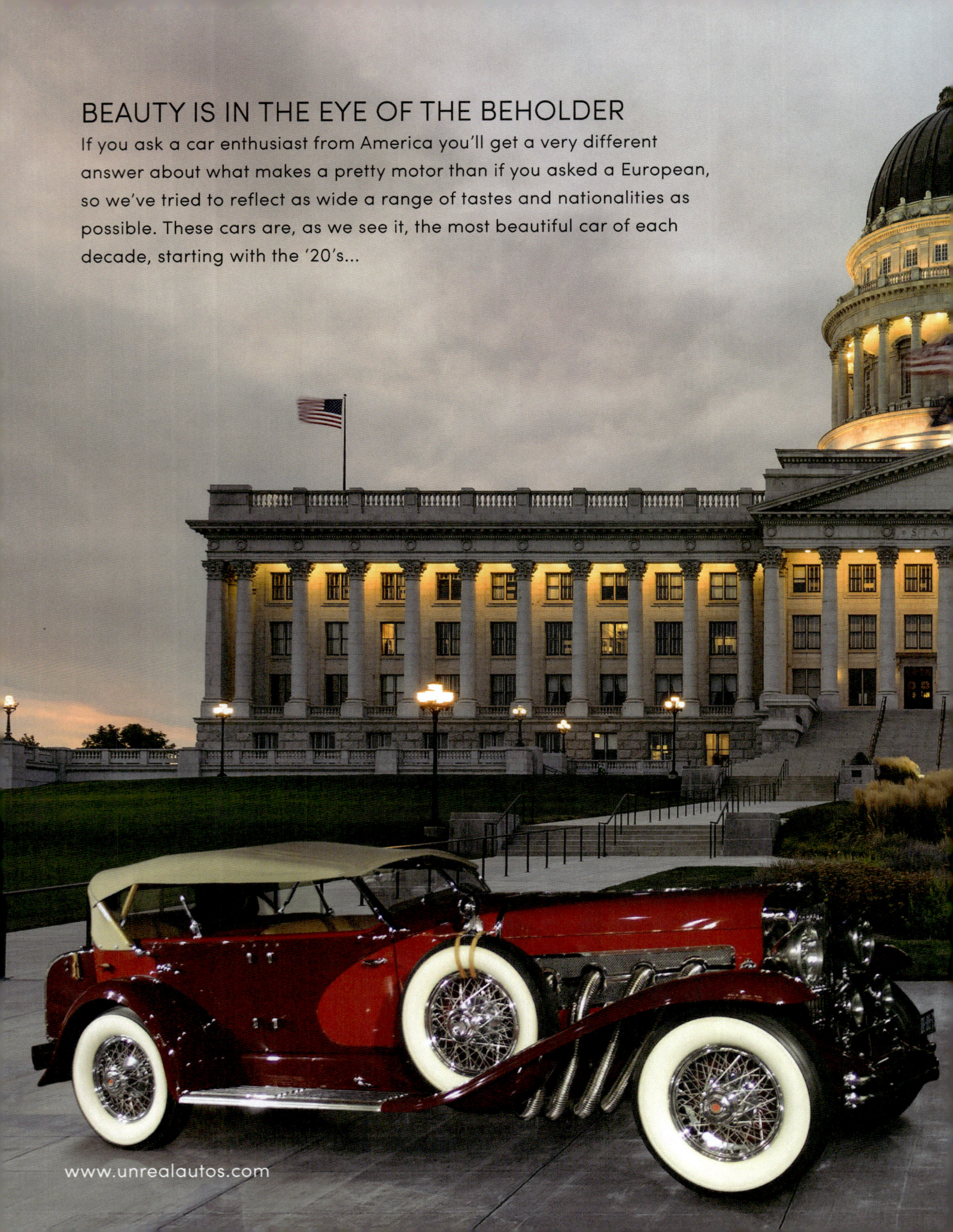

# 1920s
## DUESENBERG MODEL A (USA)

The German-American Duesenberg brothers made some classically gangsterish mobster cars in the 1930s, but they also produced some beauties in the 20s. Check out the bowtie double bumper at the front.

# 1930s
## DELAHAYE 165 (FRANCE)

In the beauty stakes, the 30s were a great time for cars. The same Art Deco movement that left its mark on the world of architecture gave us some cracking motors too. This little number is a wonderful work of art.

www.unrealautos.com

DOWNLOAD THESE PHOTOS AS
DESKTOP WALLPAPERS OR POSTERS
Go to www.unrealautos.com/wallpapers

# 1940s
## ROLLS-ROYCE PHANTOM-III VUTOTAL LABOURDETTE (UK/FRANCE)

www.unrealautos.com

Here's a car with an interesting story. Built originally by Rolls-Royce just before the outbreak of the Second World War, it was stripped and substantially rebodied by coachbuilder Labourdette of Paris after the war. With lavish embellishments costing an eye-watering $44,000 in scarce 1940s currency, the results are nothing short of breathtaking. The brass fittings catch the sun, even in an overcast England, reminding us of the golden age of automotive elegance.

www.unrealautos.com

# 1950s
## MERCEDES-BENZ 300SL (GERMANY)

The production gullwing version of this groundbreaking racing car arrived in 1955. With vertical-opening doors so iconic that Mercedes revived them many years later for the SLS, the 300SL wasn't just known for its looks. Boasting the first ever consumer fuel injection and the fastest road speeds of its day, even Ralph Lauren had to have one in his private collection. James Bond may not have driven one, but perhaps if he'd been on the big screen a few years before the DB5 arrived, he might've done. Curved to perfection!

# 1960s
## JAGUAR E-TYPE (UK)

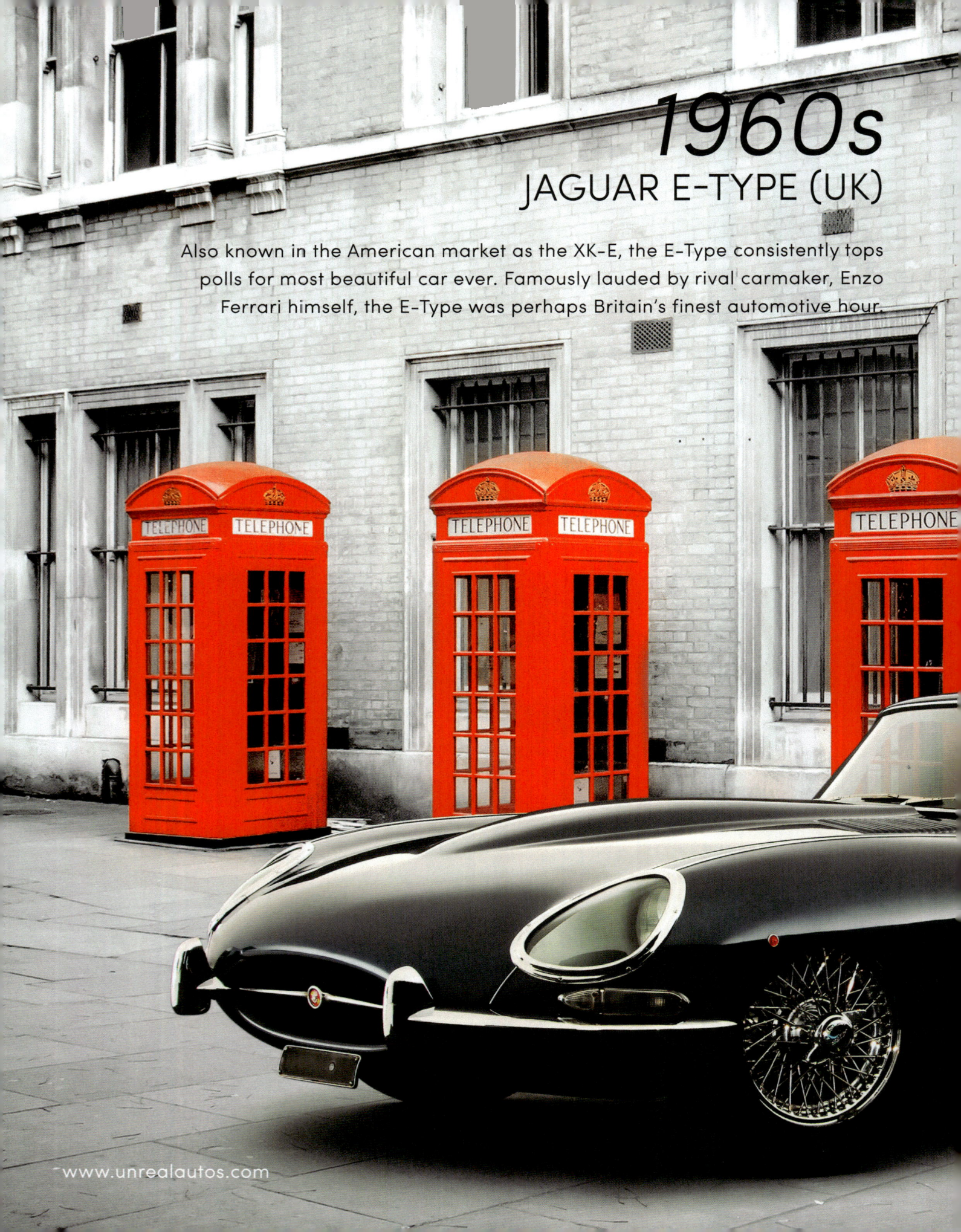

Also known in the American market as the XK-E, the E-Type consistently tops polls for most beautiful car ever. Famously lauded by rival carmaker, Enzo Ferrari himself, the E-Type was perhaps Britain's finest automotive hour.

www.unrealautos.com

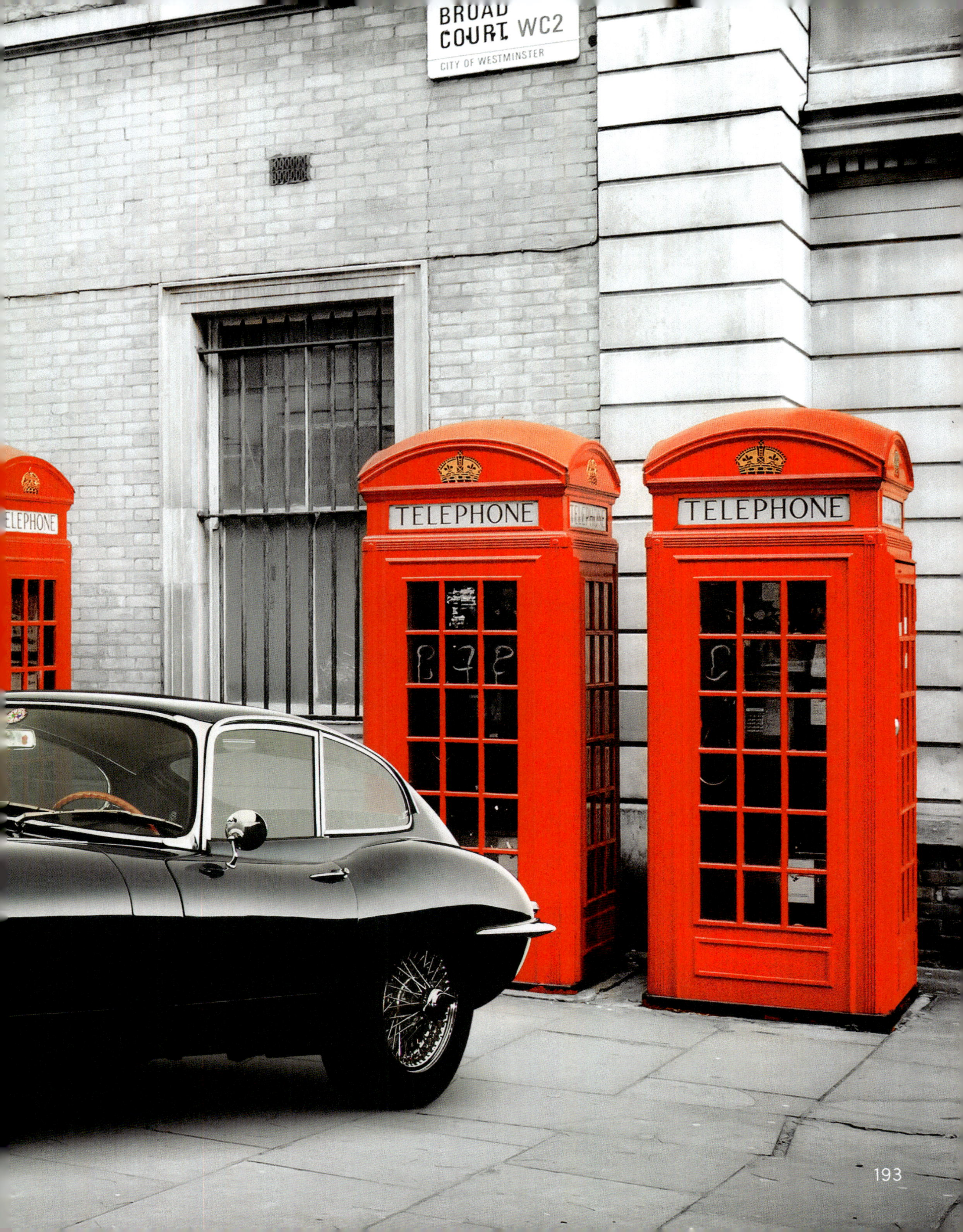
BROAD
COURT WC2
CITY OF WESTMINSTER
TELEPHONE
TELEPHONE

# 1970s
## PORSCHE 930 (GERMANY)

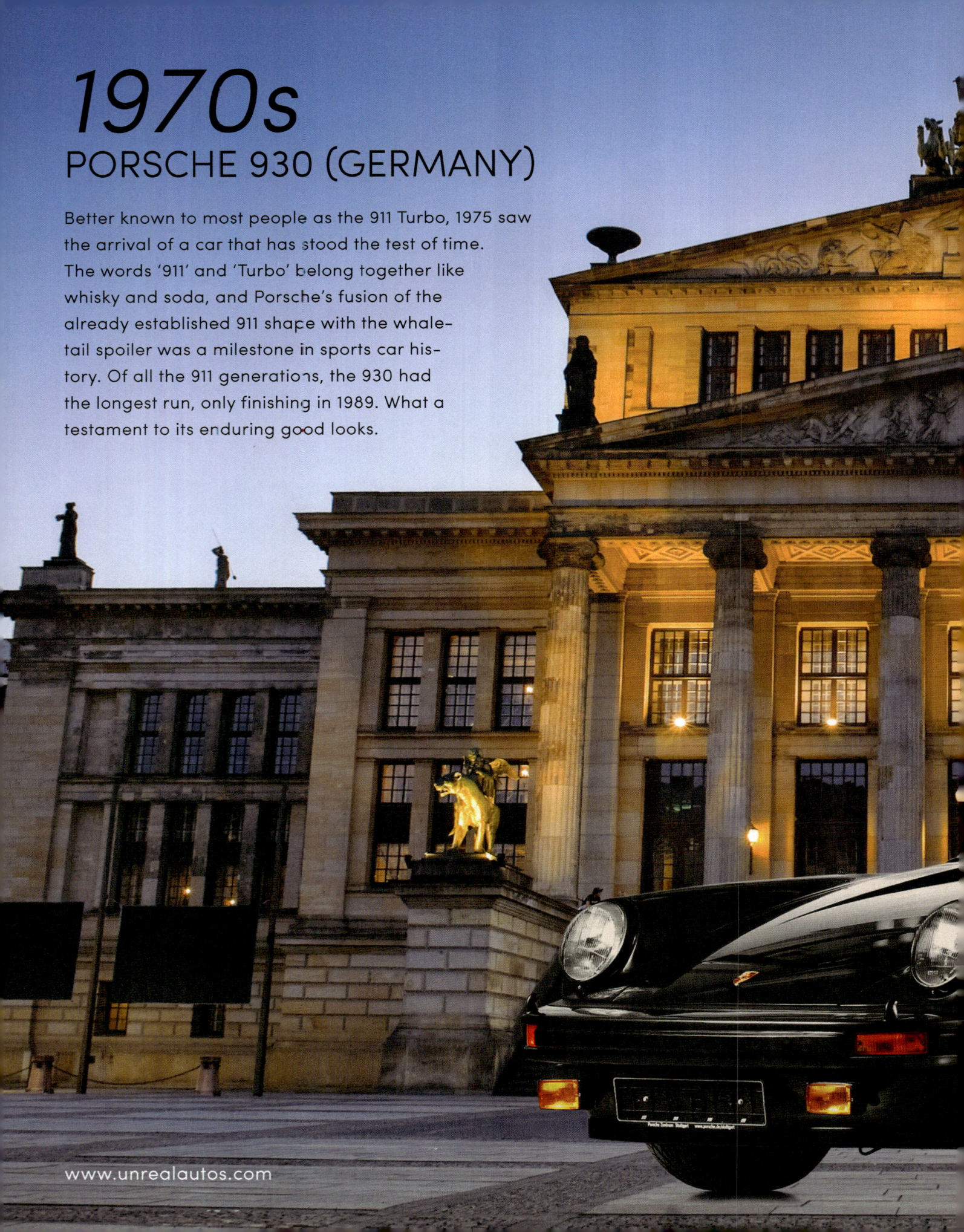

Better known to most people as the 911 Turbo, 1975 saw the arrival of a car that has stood the test of time. The words '911' and 'Turbo' belong together like whisky and soda, and Porsche's fusion of the already established 911 shape with the whale-tail spoiler was a milestone in sports car history. Of all the 911 generations, the 930 had the longest run, only finishing in 1989. What a testament to its enduring good looks.

www.unrealautos.com

195

# 1980s
## FERRARI TESTAROSSA (ITALY)

Despite the suspiciously similar 'testosterone', and despite it having a certain appeal to red-blooded men, the Testarossa apparently means 'red-head'. This beautiful beast certainly has a fiery personality.

www.unrealautos.com

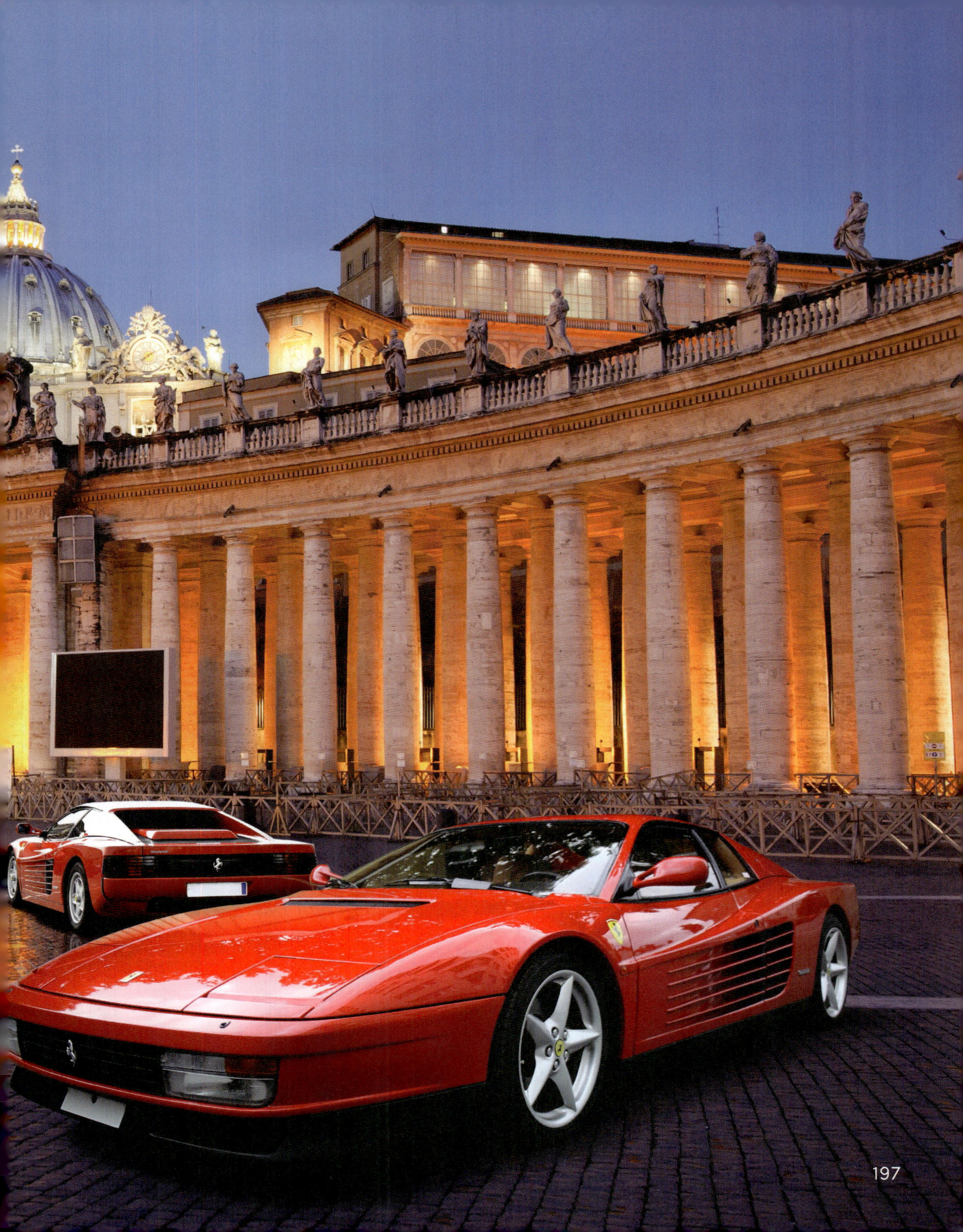

www.unrealautos.com

# 1990s
## PAGANI ZONDA (ITALY)

The Zonda C12 hit the tarmac in 1999 and took the supercar world by storm. Only replaced by the Huayra after thirteen years of production, (a car which itself holds top position in TopGear's Power Lap Table), the Zonda has style as well as speed. Named for an air current in South America, even the word Zonda just flows off the tongue, much like the wind over its exquisitely sculpted body. The boldness of some of its colour schemes was only matched by the ambition of its flamboyant designers.

www.unrealautos.com

# 2000s
## MORGAN AEROMAX (UK)

Morgan has built up a reputation for building cars that evoke the sleek lines of a bygone era whilst putting the fun back into motoring. The AeroMax first appeared in 2005, being built upon the Aero 8, but with an even better-looking front end. Now for that relaxing drive to the weekend cottage in the Cotswolds!

**DOWNLOAD THESE PHOTOS AS DESKTOP WALLPAPERS OR POSTERS**
Go to www.unrealautos.com/wallpapers

# 2010s
## LAMBORGHINI HURACÁN (ITALY)

The family resemblance may be unmistakeable but this is a Lambo of distinction. Hot off the presses as Unreal Autos went into print, the Huracán is sleeker and more elegant than the Gallardo from which it has evolved. Watch out for it at the 2014 Geneva Auto Show where it's sure to make a dramatic entrance.

www.unrealautos.com

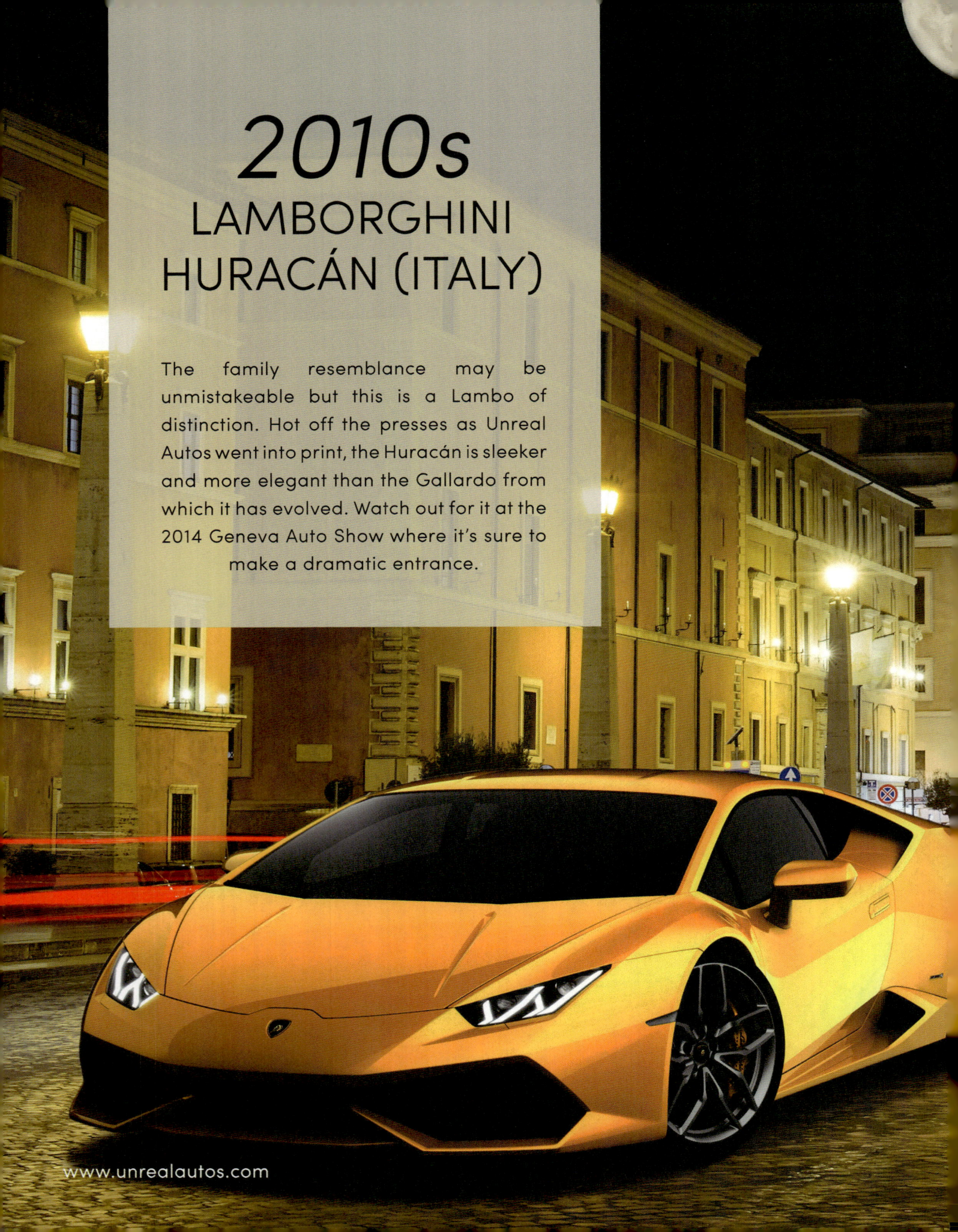

203

YOU'VE
READ THE
BOOK, NOW
DRIVE THE CARS...

Go to
www.unrealautos.com/drive

www.unrealautos.com

205

www.unrealautos.com

## TOP 10 MOST BEAUTIFUL FERRARIS OF ALL TIME

Where will you find the most exclusive gathering of Italian stallions? A clue: Look for those yellow shields. This scarlet sea of stylish European supercars is just a foretaste of what you'll find online at UnrealAutos.com. Someone once said that reds go faster, and behind the wheel of one of these for a day, you'll be able to put that to the test.

Check them out now and get your next desktop wallpaper at www.unrealautos.com.

## WHAT IS THAT CAR?

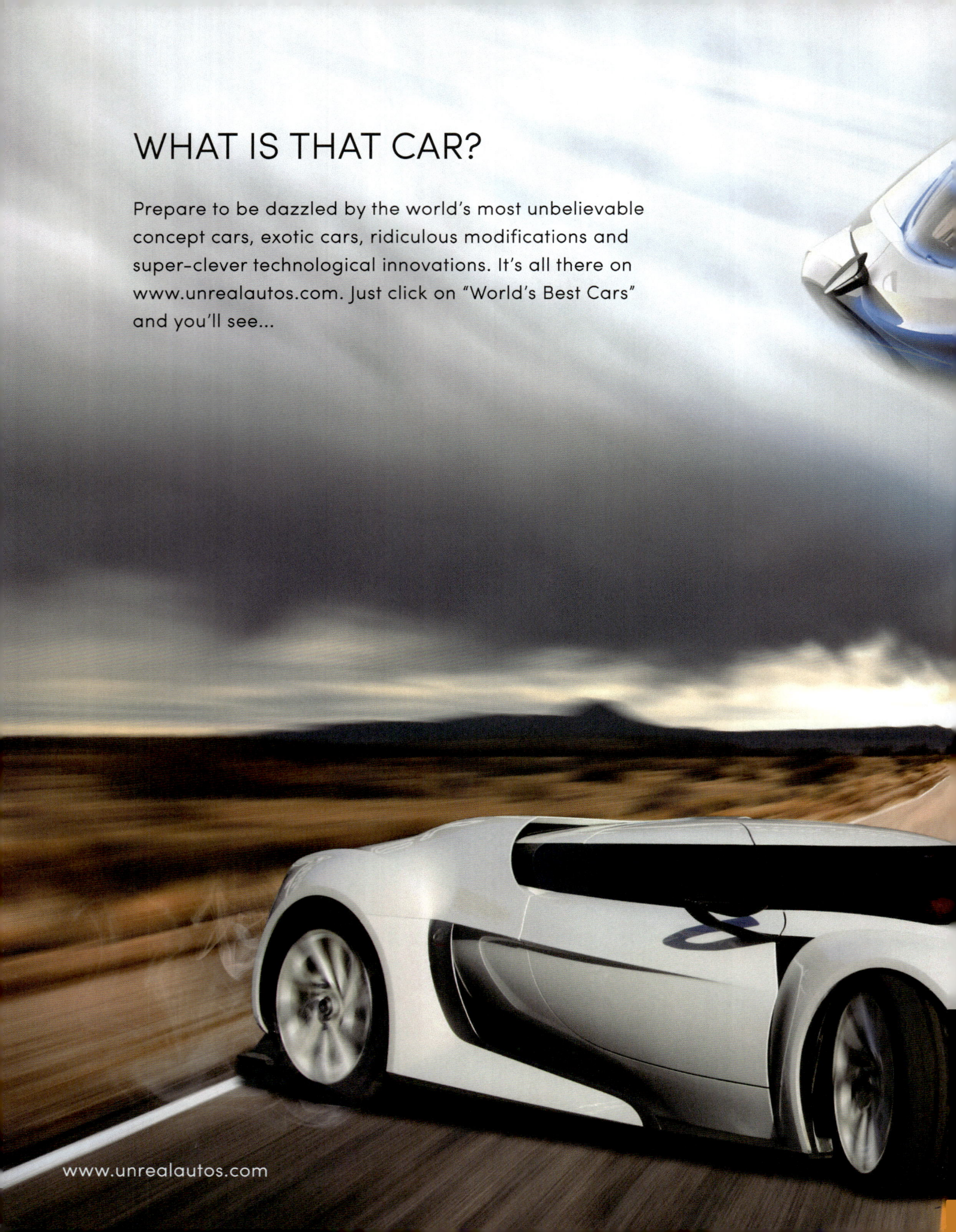

Prepare to be dazzled by the world's most unbelievable concept cars, exotic cars, ridiculous modifications and super-clever technological innovations. It's all there on www.unrealautos.com. Just click on "World's Best Cars" and you'll see...

www.unrealautos.com

CITROËN

Printed in Great Britain
by Amazon.co.uk, Ltd.,
Marston Gate.